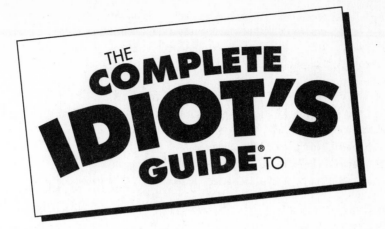

THE COMPLETE IDIOT'S GUIDE® TO

Composting

by Chris McLaughlin

ALPHA

A member of Penguin Group (USA) Inc.

This book is dedicated to my husband extraordinaire, Bobby McLaughlin, my strongest supporter who never doubted for a moment that this book would be written.

ALPHA BOOKS

Published by the Penguin Group

Penguin Group (USA) Inc., 375 Hudson Street, New York, New York 10014, USA

Penguin Group (Canada), 90 Eglinton Avenue East, Suite 700, Toronto, Ontario M4P 2Y3, Canada (a division of Pearson Penguin Canada Inc.)

Penguin Books Ltd., 80 Strand, London WC2R 0RL, England

Penguin Ireland, 25 St. Stephen's Green, Dublin 2, Ireland (a division of Penguin Books Ltd.)

Penguin Group (Australia), 250 Camberwell Road, Camberwell, Victoria 3124, Australia (a division of Pearson Australia Group Pty. Ltd.)

Penguin Books India Pvt. Ltd., 11 Community Centre, Panchsheel Park, New Delhi—110 017, India

Penguin Group (NZ), 67 Apollo Drive, Rosedale, North Shore, Auckland 1311, New Zealand (a division of Pearson New Zealand Ltd.)

Penguin Books (South Africa) (Pty.) Ltd., 24 Sturdee Avenue, Rosebank, Johannesburg 2196, South Africa

Penguin Books Ltd., Registered Offices: 80 Strand, London WC2R 0RL, England

International Standard Book Number: 978-1-61564-008-9
Library of Congress Catalog Card Number: 2009938586

12 11 10   8 7 6 5 4 3 2 1

Interpretation of the printing code: The rightmost number of the first series of numbers is the year of the book's printing; the rightmost number of the second series of numbers is the number of the book's printing. For example, a printing code of 10-1 shows that the first printing occurred in 2010.

Printed in the United States of America

Note: This publication contains the opinions and ideas of its author. It is intended to provide helpful and informative material on the subject matter covered. It is sold with the understanding that the author and publisher are not engaged in rendering professional services in the book. If the reader requires personal assistance or advice, a competent professional should be consulted.

The author and publisher specifically disclaim any responsibility for any liability, loss, or risk, personal or otherwise, which is incurred as a consequence, directly or indirectly, of the use and application of any of the contents of this book.

Most Alpha books are available at special quantity discounts for bulk purchases for sales promotions, premiums, fundraising, or educational use. Special books, or book excerpts, can also be created to fit specific needs.

For details, write: Special Markets, Alpha Books, 375 Hudson Street, New York, NY 10014.

Publisher: *Marie Butler-Knight*
Editorial Director: *Mike Sanders*
Senior Managing Editor: *Billy Fields*
Acquisitions Editor: *Tom Stevens*
Development Editor: *Jennifer Moore*
Senior Production Editor: *Janette Lynn*
Copy Editor: *Jan Zoya*

Cartoonist: *Hollis McLaughlin*
Cover Designer: *Bill Thomas*
Book Designer: *Trina Wurst*
Indexer: *Brad Herriman*
Layout: *Rebecca Batchelor, Brian Massey*
Proofreader: *Laura Caddell*

Contents at a Glance

Contents

Introduction

Gardens are once again coming into vogue. And as more people start to grow their own vegetables, they are beginning to recognize the value of high-quality soil that's packed with nutrients. The better your soil is, the healthier and more fruitful your plants will be. In other words, build it and they will come. This is where composting comes in.

Composting is both the art and science of blending organic materials with water and air so that the nutrition in the organic matter decomposes into a plant-useable form called humus.

Unfortunately, much of the information about composting you find in magazines and books, while accurate, is unnecessarily complicated. Discerning the carbon to nitrogen ratio every time you toss materials into your compost pile, measuring pH levels, and taking the pile's temperature are absolutely optional activities.

The truth is that composting is about as simple as it gets. Anyone with a spare half hour and some organic material lying around can begin to reap its benefits. It's not rocket science. You don't need to wait for a particular time of year to get started. You don't need to buy any expensive supplies. And you don't need to do a lick of math.

The key is to have some information on hand (this book), decide what kind of container or bin you'd like to use, then go outside and start a pile. You can create a perfectly adequate pile in 30 minutes—and usually less. But if you're like most people, once you start reaping the benefits of your first simple pile, you'll be eager to try your hand at different techniques in an effort to get as much compost as you can, as quickly as you can. This book is intended to grow with you and your garden as you explore the many ways to turn organic waste materials into garden gold.

How This Book Is Organized

The Complete Idiot's Guide® to Composting is divided into three parts.

Part 1, "The Dirt Beneath Your Feet," tells you everything you need to know about composting. You'll learn what supplies you'll need, what you can put into your pile, and approximately how long it will be before you'll have a beautiful pile of garden gold to spread in your vegetable and herb gardens and flower beds.

Part 2, "Worm Wrangling 101: Vermicomposting," is intended to get you hooked on worms (pun intended). You might be cringing now, but after reading about the benefits of worm farming (vermicomposting), you'll never look at worms the same way again. Worm castings are the crème de la crème of the composting world.

Part 3, "Creative Composting: Beyond the Bin," describes other composting techniques that are just as beneficial for your soil as traditional composting. You'll learn about sandwich composting, grasscyling, mulching, and growing cover crops. Although the process may be different, all of these techniques have one thing in common: they add valuable nutrients to the soil.

More Cool Stuff

Along the way you'll find the following extras:

Digging Deeper
Here you'll find tips and advice on putting your composting techniques to work.

Wise Worm
These sidebars contain fun and informative facts.

Prickly Problem
Read these sidebars to find out how to avoid composting catastrophes.

def•i•ni•tion
These sidebars provide definitions and details about specific composting and gardening terms and techniques.

Acknowledgments

While no one should have to put up with writers, these guys managed it and, more importantly, without strangling me. The first person I want to thank is my fantabulous editor, Tom Stevens, who has so much patience it's disturbing. Alpha Books and Penguin Group for putting together a series of books that are not only bursting with information and great fun to read, but also a joy to write. My agent, Marilyn Allen, who went to bat for me on little more than faith. I thank, from the bottom of my heart, Karen Berger for being kind enough to loan me her agent and Julie Haas-Wajdowicz for being my professional eye and letting me exhale. A big thank you to the rest of the editing team, Jennifer Moore and Jan Zoya.

A *huge* thank-you to Penny Warner, who's my favorite author in the entire world and a most gracious teacher. Joe Lamp'l for his kindness and generosity. Angela England for kicking my butt and making me stay the course. I'm indebted to Leslie Carlsen, Alana Inugai, and Colleen Vanderlinden for their cheerleading skills. Deanne Gossler who stays as far away from dirt as possible but tried very hard to look like she was compelled by microbes and compost turners. My sister-in-law Cindy who is also very gifted at hiding her glazed eyes. Thanks also to Alex Jansen for bringing Fred #422 to life as the Wise Worm in this book.

I must mention how special it was to create a book that features the wonderful artwork by my daughter, Hollis McLaughlin, who drew things exactly as I wanted them to look (like a good kid). Brittany Reynolds, who is perhaps the only person capable of holding down the fort while I'm in hiding. Thanks to Hunter McLaughlin for being a brutal in-house editor and Bella McLaughlin for being patient and giving up time with her mom so this book could be written. Jillian Reynolds who was a big surprise and an even bigger joy.

Thanks also go to Tony Deffina and Mike Deffina, who also chose to walk down creative paths. I'm eternally thankful to my mom, Jeani Deffina, who gave me my love for the written word and taught me how to drink in books. My dad, Michael Deffina, who just might be one of my biggest fans—I know that I am his. My parents gave me permission to have complete and utter drive for my passions, and that's made all the difference. My biggest thank you has to go out to Bobby, who never complained once and who's become one hell of a cook.

I can't leave out the irreplaceable Mrs. Greenthumbs, Cassandra Danz, for teaching me that gardening books can be fantastic reads and gardens are mostly about sex.

It's a privilege to have every one of you in my life.

Special Thanks to the Technical Reviewer

The Complete Idiot's Guide to Composting was reviewed by an expert who double-checked the accuracy of what you'll learn here, to help us ensure that this book gives you everything you need to know about composting. Special thanks are extended to Julie Haas-Wajdowicz.

Trademarks

All terms mentioned in this book that are known to be or are suspected of being trademarks or service marks have been appropriately capitalized. Alpha Books and Penguin Group (USA) Inc. cannot attest to the accuracy of this information. Use of a term in this book should not be regarded as affecting the validity of any trademark or service mark.

Part 1

The Dirt Beneath Your Feet

We walk on it our entire lives. We pave over it, drive on it, dig in it, remove it—and if we're smart, we'll replenish it. Yet most people, most of the time, don't give the earth beneath their feet a second thought. That is, until the day they decide to grow plants in it and their garden fails to thrive. That's the day when most of us start taking a long, hard look at the soil and realize that there's something missing. Exactly what *is* good garden soil? Why do gardeners take so much pride in a handful of crumbly dirt?

Making compost is one of the easiest and least expensive ways to add nutrients and structure to your soil. In the following chapters you'll find out exactly what's in that "garden gold" and why it's so good for your garden and landscape beds. You'll see just how easy it is to create beautiful, life-giving humus. Composting will make your plants healthier and your garden more productive. Soon, you won't be happy until you have a big pile for yourself!

It's Alive!

In This Chapter

- ◆ Making beautiful soil
- ◆ Composting as a good hobby
- ◆ Saving time and money
- ◆ Warding off diseases and extending your growing season
- ◆ Dispelling composting myths

If you'd like healthier plants, higher produce yields, and fewer garden diseases, the place to concentrate on is your soil. Garden soil's best friend is compost. The aim of this chapter is to get you all fired up about composting by explaining its many benefits as well as dispelling some of the myths surrounding the process.

What the Heck *Is* Soil, Anyway?

The first thing you need to know about soil is that it's not dead. Soil is full of billions and billions of living and breathing organisms that are invisible to the human eye. In the simplest of terms, soil is made up of organic matter, minerals, water, and air. All of these ingredients not only make up a stable medium for roots to hang on to but also provide for plants' nutritional needs.

As a gardener, you'll probably only need one season to realize that the key to healthy, productive plants is soil that's rich in organic matter. *Organic matter* is the very heart of compost, and its final result—humus. Composting is sustainability at its finest for plants and the other living organisms on this planet.

People usually use the word "dirt" as a generic term for soil or as a derogatory label for soil that doesn't have much going for it in the way of nutritional value. Either way, most gardeners prefer to use the term "soil" when referring to the nutritionally rich garden earth.

def•i•ni•tion

Organic matter is any material that originates from living organisms, including all animal and plant life whether still living or in any stage of decomposition.

The Components of Good Garden Soil

Compost is the finished product of broken-down organic plant and animal matter. In its "finished" form, compost becomes *humus*. Humus is compost that can't be broken down any further—in short, it's gardener nirvana. Excellent soil that's full of life-sustaining humus is often called "friable," meaning that it has a full, loamy texture and crumbles easily in your hands.

def•i•ni•tion

Humus is the product of degraded plant and animal matter that has nearly completely broken down. Humus is compost at its richest in organic matter. It makes complex nutrients in the soil easily accessible to plants.

Compost can add any number of nutrients to the soil depending on what materials are added to the compost pile. Other micronutrients that add value to the compost (therefore, the garden soil) are copper, iron, iodine, zinc, manganese, cobalt, boron, and molybdenum. I don't recommend trying to measure organic matter in order to ensure these nutrients are in there. However, it makes good sense, then, to add as wide a variety of materials to your compost pile as you can.

Why Decomposition Is a Good Hobby

While humus is the ultimate goal, you can use compost in garden beds at any time during the composting process. For instance, compost at any stage can be used as mulch by retaining moisture, suppressing weeds, and as erosion control.

Compost adds value to soil by providing it with nitrogen, phosphorus, potassium, and other minerals. It can also eliminate the need for synthetic fertilizers and ward off plant diseases.

Synthetic fertilizers may temporarily mask the problem of poor soil by perking plants up with some green, but they don't actually solve the problem permanently. Compost, on the other hand, changes the structure of the soil, making it nutritionally rich.

Compost can be applied to soils in just about as many ways as your imagination will allow. Some gardeners stick to the traditional way of letting their compost pile "cook" and then adding it all at once to their garden beds. But it can also be used as a side-dressing and as a potting mix for outdoor potted plants or house plants. Compost doesn't have to be created in a bin or pile; you can compost in a trench next to the planted veggies or build a layered compost pile and plant directly into it. You'll learn about the many composting possibilities in upcoming chapters.

Although gardeners usually take full credit for their compost, they are really stealing much of the credit from Mother Nature. Nature doesn't need help composting organic materials, but you can act as an accelerator. In reality, what's really going on here is the same natural decomposition that has happened on the ground since time began.

Gardeners speed up the process by organizing the percentage of individual ingredients in such a way that they get their precious garden gold as fast as nature will allow. Because, with or without us, compost happens.

The following sections outline some of other benefits of composting.

Wise Worm

Fertile soil is bursting with life. There are approximately 5 billion people in the world, which is about the same number of critters you can find in a single handful of soil. Bacteria accounts for much of that number as they're the most plentiful creatures on Earth.

Composting Suppresses Diseases

Researchers have discovered another virtue of compost that doesn't get as much publicity as it should: it's valuable for plant-disease resistance. The beneficial microorganisms produced by composting organic materials render plant pathogens inactive. Potato blight, powdery mildew, and damping off are all examples of plant diseases that compost can suppress.

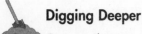

Digging Deeper _____

Compost lets air circulate easily due to the light crumb structure of humus. Oxygen is necessary to create a healthy environment for plant roots and beneficial microbes living in the soil. A crumblike structure also makes the soil easy to work.

Composting Increases the Growing Season

Composted soils enable the gardener to plant earlier in the growing season and harvest later in the season. Compost improves average soil structure by bringing it to a loamy, friable state. Nutritionally rich soil with good structure is able to hold heat better than poor soil. For the gardener, this means the soil warms up faster and stays warm longer.

Composting Serves as a pH Buffer

Soil pH is a measure of soil's acidity or alkalinity. For most plants, the most desirable pH is neutral—neither too acidic nor too alkaline. To determine a soil's pH, you usually have to do a soil test yourself with a kit or send a soil sample off to your local agricultural extension office. But if you're generous with applying compost to your garden soil, you don't have to worry about the pH levels as much—if at all!

When humus is plentiful in soil, vegetable crops and flower beds are simply less dependent on pH levels in the soil. Due to its biochemical structure, humus acts as a buffer for soils that fall slightly to one side of acidic or alkaline. This not only takes the guesswork out of an average pH level, but it can take the pH factor out of the equation entirely.

Of course, if your garden has been under a pile of pine needles for 20 years, the soil will be highly acidic. In that case, you'll certainly want to consider spreading an amendment, such as lime, on it to bring the soil closer to neutral. After that, just add as much compost as you can to the garden bed. You may also want to avoid adding acidic materials, such as citrus peelings or pine needles, to the compost bin until you know you've eliminated the imbalance.

Composting Is Good for the Earth

When people compost, they reduce the amount of waste that would otherwise end up in landfills or dumps. The greenhouse gasses produced by landfills don't actually *stay* in the landfills. Instead, the gasses escape into the atmosphere, contributing to global warming.

Kitchen waste, cardboard, paper, and yard or grass clippings—all ideal compost ingredients—make up two thirds of the garbage Americans toss out each year. Even more surprising is the fact that we purchase expensive soil amendments, bagged mulch, and premixed mediums for our gardens and landscape.

The "garbage" we're tossing out is the very thing that could be creating the very stuff we're out there buying! A whopping 75 percent of the organic resources (compostable stuff) can be put right back into our yards and the earth, where they're the most valuable.

Composting also helps create a healthy environment for wildlife. Wildlife has been dealt a raw hand due to the degradation and loss of habitat. By amending your soil with compost, you'll bring with it *microorganisms* and *macroorganisms* that support all wild animals and plants. In addition, because composting reduces the need for chemical herbicides and pesticides, you'll automatically be making your garden a more environmentally friendly place.

def•i•ni•tion

Microorganisms, also called microbes, are organisms, such as bacteria and fungi, that can't be seen with the naked eye. They're the world's smallest life forms and are essential to every life form in the world.

Macroorganisms are critters that *are* visible to people; they help break down larger pieces of organic material so the microbes can finish composting them.

Composting Saves Time

Compost increases soil's capacity to hold water by a wide margin. For instance, a dry soil low in nutrients may only hold 20 percent of its weight in water. Compare this to a dry soil that's high in organic content, which can hold up to 200 percent of its weight in water. Composting your soil means that you'll need to spend less time watering.

And here's another time saver: when used as mulch, compost not only helps to suppress weeds, but makes them easier to pull out if they do show up.

Composting Saves Money

Composting offers so much nutritional value to plants that you may never need to purchase commercial fertilizers again. This is, indeed, the ultimate goal of many gardeners.

Due to its super water-holding capabilities, you'll water composted garden beds less, which translates to a lower water bill.

After you've been composting for a while, you begin to get a real feel for what you can put in your pile. By composting as many organic materials that you can, you use less space in your garbage cans, which means a lower garbage bill.

Remember the weed control that mulching with compost provides? You'll not only save time, but you'll save money by not having to purchase chemical weed controls.

Wise Worm _____

The nutrients in organic waste matter are unreachable to plants in their original form. The decomposition of organic material converts the nutrients of dead plant and animal tissues into forms that can be easily absorbed by plants.

Composting Reduces Water Run-Off

Due to the poor crumb structure of soil that's low in organic matter, it can be washed away easily by storms or even everyday watering. Lost topsoil results in even lower fertility, creating a vicious cycle. Compost preserves and enhances soil structure and helps fight erosion, keeping healthy soil under the plants where it belongs.

Composting Myths

Unfortunately, composting sometimes gets a bad rap. When people cite reasons for not composting, they often roll out one of the following composting myths. Fortunately, most of these myths turn out to be blatantly false; others have a ring of truth to them, but the issue is usually easily addressed. Let's start with one of the most common composting myths out there …

Compost piles smell bad. In the several years I've been composting, I've never had a bad-smelling compost pile. I know if you try hard, you can create a bad-smelling pile, but honestly, it doesn't take much to keep it as nature intended—fresh like the forest floor.

Organic matter that's composting has a woodsy smell. It is entirely possible to put ingredients together in a way that encourages bad bacteria to move into the pile and give it a bad odor. But even then the problem can be easily addressed by adding some carbon such as paper or leaves, or by simply turning the pile over.

Smelly piles are usually the result of too much nitrogen—such as a thick layer of grass clippings—or the inclusion of meat or dairy waste. The solution would be to add carbon materials and turn the pile over. If animal products end up in the pile, you'll need to either turn the pile or remove the offending waste.

Another reason for unpleasant odors is too much moisture. Excess water might make the pile anaerobic, which can be remedied by adding some browns and aerating the pile.

Composting is expensive. The only part of composting that might possibly be costly is if you run out and buy an expensive composting bin. And there are pricey bins on the market—some costing hundreds of dollars! The good news is that you don't have to purchase any kind of compost bin. In Chapter 5, I show you so many ways to contain your compost on the cheap that you're going to wonder how the compost bin guys stay in business! But there are good reasons why they do, and I'll explain that, too.

Composting is complicated. Some people think that they need to be a math major with a minor in engineering in order to compost correctly. After all, creating good soil is all about measuring and science, right? Wrong again. You don't have to do a single calculation to create gorgeous soil for your garden. In this book, I show you how to leave the science to the ultimate expert—Mother Nature. *We* are going to practice art.

You need a lot of land or open space to compost correctly. Another rumor that doesn't hold water. People who live in apartments and condominiums are perfectly capable of composting. All they need is a small tumbling bin, a plain garbage can, or a vermicomposting system (more on these in later chapters).

You need to add special compost activators or starters. While it can be nice to toss in a commercial activator to get things going, in no way is doing so a necessity. In fact, I've never used one in my pile, and I have some fast-producing piles. For people who want to give some store-bought stuff a shot, it's available; otherwise, Mother Nature does it right.

Composting takes a lot of time and effort. You have to be a true work horse to keep a compost pile hot and moving. Ummmm … wrong again! I'm a fairly lazy composter. I certainly don't work hard at it, and compost happens.

It's a simple give-and-take proposition. You gather the goods necessary to decompose organic materials and pile it up. Turn it once in a while and nature will do the rest. Promise.

Undesirable animals are attracted to compost piles. Okay, I have to concede this one. If a gardener has added dairy products, meat, fat, or the like, then rats, raccoons, dogs, and stray cats will almost certainly make their way to your pile and dig around looking for Friday night's takeout. Sometimes raccoons or even the family dog will even go for veggie or fruit scraps in a compost pile. This is why I urge gardeners to only add the appropriate kitchen scraps to enclosed compost bins such as tumblers or plastic ones with four sides and a secure lid. An open pile should be loaded only with yard wastes and nonfood items.

Digging Deeper

The difference between decomposition at landfills and decomposition in a compost pile at home is *how* the organic matter decomposes. At landfills, over half of the gases produced during decomposition are methane-based greenhouse gases due to the lack of oxygen. In home compost piles, carbon dioxide is produced rather than methane, as the compost decays from oxygen. Even a cold compost pile at home usually receives ample oxygen due to occasional turning, worms, and other macrobial organisms within the pile. This results in a huge reduction of greenhouse gases.

Humus: The Final Frontier

For gardens, humus is the proverbial pot of gold at the end of the composting rainbow. And there are many ways to end up with a big pot of the gardening nirvana. It all depends on what individual gardeners have on hand while the pile is being built and turned.

Composts vary in mineral content and pH levels. But for the most part, if a wide variety of organic materials is tossed into the pile, the finished compost or humus is going to be pretty close to as balanced and stable as anything you could buy commercially.

Keep in mind that not all composting techniques work for everybody. Start with the system that best fits your lifestyle. Ignore anyone who tells you it has to be a certain way. Look at it this way: if you let people convince you to compost in a way that doesn't work for you and your family, you'll probably stop composting altogether.

The goal is to use the organic materials you have on hand and pile them in a way that works for you so you can reap the many rewards of composting.

The Least You Need to Know

- ◆ Soil is a living, breathing entity.

- ◆ Compost happens—with or without human involvement.

- ◆ Compost is a great disease suppressor; season extender; pH buffer; time- , money- , and water-saver; and, it's awesome for the earth!

- ◆ Composting doesn't smell, isn't complicated, and can be done very inexpensively.

- ◆ You can create compost using any one of numerous formulas and systems. Find one that works for you.

2

It's Only Fourth Grade Science

In This Chapter

- ◆ The microbial and macrobial decomposers
- ◆ Carbon vs. nitrogen
- ◆ Why water and air are important
- ◆ Compost activators

Composting is no less than an incredible transformation of organic material into a rich nutrient source for plants.

This chapter explains how that transformation takes place. Although you certainly don't need to know the science behind composting in order to get started, I am confident that you will find the process fascinating. So sit back, relax, and enjoy. And if you skim ahead or doze off, no worries—compost happens even when you're not paying attention.

Meet the Decomposers

Unfortunately, many of the organisms that are necessary for good compost—bacteria, bugs, worms, and fungi—don't sound particularly interesting or attractive. Creatures that make things rot and decay have had a negative connotation.

I'd like to show you how *decomposers* are not only fascinating but are, in fact, *essential* for life here on Earth. So let me introduce you to some of your wriggly, squirmy, and hard-working composting crew.

def•i•ni•tion

Decomposer is a general term for any organism that breaks down organic materials to provide nutrients for plants. The term describes microorganisms as well as macroorganisms.

Key Microbial Decomposers: Critters You Can't See

Microorganisms do twice the work of an *Extreme Makeover* construction crew. They're the most valuable contributor to rich, dark humus. But because they are invisible to the naked eye, you've got to have a little faith, as you can't actually see them at work. These tiny heroes of humus include bacteria, fungi, and actinomycetes.

Wise Worm

Bacteria are found on every living creature and are one of the most essential life forms on Earth. And although we usually associate bacteria with disease, many bacteria actually prevent illness. Here's a little tidbit that will keep you up at night: bacteria on the human body outnumber human cells 10 to 1!

Bacteria

Bacteria are by far the most plentiful microorganisms in compost piles, constituting as much as 90 percent of the population. And although there may be thousands of specific bacteria in a pile, they all fall into three general categories:

- Psychrophiles
- Mesophiles
- Thermophiles

Psychrophiles are often the first to make themselves at home in your smorgasbord of a compost pile. These little organisms are comfortable at temperatures ranging from 30°F to 55°F. During the cold months of winter, it's primarily these characters that are working away at your compost.

The psychrophiles consume the organic matter and release amino acids into the pile. At this point, things really begin to heat up—literally—as the bacteria give off some of their energy as heat.

From the outside looking in, it seems that the heat is what's breaking down the pile. Actually, the heat itself doesn't aid in the breakdown of the organic matter, but it does create a hospitable environment in which other organisms can thrive. When any condition in a compost pile changes, such as the moisture or temperature, different microbes begin to move in and set up home. Soon, there'll be a whole new community of active workers (decomposers) in the pile.

Mesophiles are the next bacterial group to join the decomposition party. Mesos are present in compost temperatures between 50°F and 113°F, although, like people, they perform their best in temps of 70°F to 90°F. Decomposition at this point is cruising along at a decent clip. When temperatures reach over 100 degrees, the mesophiles begin to die off.

The mesophiles have been touted by some microbiologists as having superior efficiency to the next group, the thermophiles. They are the unsung heroes of the compost pile, doing most of the composition work but getting little of the credit.

However, mesophilic bacteria lack the turbo power to kill off weed seeds effectively, nor do they kill organisms that cause disease. Enter the thermophiles—our most serious partiers.

Thermophiles thrive in the now-cooking compost pile. A pile typically reaches a peak temperature of around 160°F, but normally this lasts for less than a week at a time. As the environment changes due to weather conditions and what you add to the heap on any given day, the temperature of the compost heap changes as well.

Fungi and Actinomycetes

Think of fungi and actinomycetes (*ac-ti-no-MY-set-ees*) as the "finishing school" for compost. They polish off what the bacteria started. Woody and fibrous organic materials are tough customers to break down, and these guys are just the right microbes for the job. Fungi work shoulder to shoulder with the psychrophiles in the cooler temperatures.

You might also notice white, fuzzy stuff in your pile that prefers to hang around the mesophiles—these are the actinomycetes. When the core temps of the pile get too hot, they'll loiter around the outer parameters of the compost party like high school freshmen.

Things begin to feel oh-so-right when the actinomycetes show up because they're responsible for that fresh, earthy scent (think forest floor) of curing compost piles. These dudes have a foothold in both the fungus and bacterial camps, as it's actually a half-breed comprised of both. Sometimes people confuse actinomycetes with mold, which is green rather than white. Even mold is a welcome employee in the compost pile as a helpful decomposer.

Key Macrobial Decomposers: Critters You *Can* See

Along with the invisible bacterial microbes, the macrobial decomposers also take up residence inside your compost pile. The bigger, and therefore visible, decomposers work in tandem with the microbials and are just as valuable for decomposition. You'll recognize most of these critters as millipedes, centipedes, redworms, night crawlers, spiders, nematodes, snails, ants, grubs, springtails, beetles, mites, sow bugs, and pill bugs (roly polies).

These larger critters break down pieces of organic material, exposing more surface area for the microbes to finish their work. These invertebrates consume and mix together the organic material in the pile. Worms perform double duty by aerating the soil by tunneling through it, while their rich, organic excrement further enhances the compost. Worms are such effective composters that they get three entire chapters devoted to them (see Part 2).

In order for the microbial and macrobial decomposers to work quickly and efficiently, they need four basic things: carbon, nitrogen, water, and oxygen (air). Let's take a closer look at each of them.

Meet the Browns: Carbon

Think of your compost critters as any other living creature. They're going to need food for energy in the form of carbohydrates. Here's where the browns (carbon) come in. Compost is created when microbes and macrobes eat the carbon and nitrogen that you provide in your compost pile. While ingesting the carbon materials, they're also getting phosphorus and a handful of other necessary elements.

All organic matter is composed of both carbon and nitrogen; however, some material is far heavier on the carbon side of the equation, and these are what we refer to as "browns." For example, straw's carbon-to-nitrogen ratio is about 80:1; that's 80 parts carbon to 1 part nitrogen. Corn stalks and leaves are about 60:1, sawdust is 500:1, and paper is 170:1.

Most carbon-type matter appears brown like leaves or cardboard. If you feel your pile is lacking in carbon materials, don't forget all the paper goods in your house such as your old bills, school notices, newspapers, and cardboard.

Another potential source of carbon that's overlooked is 100 percent cotton fabrics and dryer lint. Cotton fabric scraps, old T-shirts, or what have you, can be cut up and tossed right into the compost pile.

The following list includes examples of carbon-rich materials you may find around your yard and home:

Wise Worm

The nutrients in organic waste matter are unreachable to plants in their original forms. The decomposition of organic material converts the nutrients of the dead tissues into a form that's easily accessible to plants.

Aged hay	Dryer lint
*Dried leaves (shredded)	Cardboard
Sawdust	Cardboard egg cartons
Chipped wood	Newspaper
Toilet paper rolls	Paper towels
Dried grasses	Wrapping paper
Straw	Oat hay
Wood ash (not coal ash)	Shredded documents
100% cotton fabrics	

*A note about dried leaves: While certainly it's fine to add some, you'll want to be sure they're quite shredded (a lawn mower works well) and you don't have so many that they form a thick mass, because they don't decompose well in that state. If you have a large quantity of dried leaves, make a separate compost pile to create leaf mold, which we'll go over in Chapter 6.

Some gardeners don't like to add wood ash to their composts regularly because it can raise soil pH levels. But added in moderation, wood ash is a good source of potassium (potash) for compost. This not only helps plants fight disease, but also makes their tissues stronger. Plants also need potash to produce chlorophyll, which plays a key role in photosynthesis.

Meet the Greens: Nitrogen

Just as our composting critters need carbon for energy, they also need nitrogen, or "greens," for growth and reproduction. To fulfill the green requirement, you'll need to feed them nitrogen-rich organic materials whose carbon-to-nitrogen (C:N) ratios fall lower than 30 on the C side of the equation. An example of an organic material high in nitrogen is grass, usually added to the pile in the form of clippings; these are about 20:1—that is, 20 parts carbon to 1 part nitrogen. While the first number (the carbon) sounds high compared to the nitrogen number, you have to remember that the perfect C:N ratio is 30:1. If your carbon number is higher than 30, the material is considered a carbon product; if it's lower than 30, it's a nitrogen product.

Prickly Problem

When adding wood ash to the compost pile or bin the gardener must be certain that the ashes are completely cooled. Hot embers should never be put into the compost pile as they can easily become a fire hazard.

Because the carbon number in grass clippings is cruising below 30, the clippings are packed with nitrogen. Their disposition is considered "green." Kitchen scraps are about 15:1 and rotted manure is around 25:1. All of these materials are nitrogen rich and a key component to the compost pile.

Just like browns, greens are everywhere. You'll be amazed at the everyday stuff you can use as a basic nitrogen food source for your pile. Here's a list of common nitrogen-rich materials:

Green grass clippings	Kelp/seaweed
Vegetable trimmings	Algae
Green leaves	Aquarium water (freshwater)
Tea bags (the bag, too)	Alfalfa meal or hay
Coffee grounds (and filter)	Citrus*
Animal manure (herbivores)	Houseplants

Weeds (without seeds)   Old flower bouquets

Human and animal hair   Green prunings

Grass clippings from your lawn are loaded with nitrogen and do beautiful work heating up your compost pile. They add phosphorus and potassium, as well. If you store them until they turn brown, they become a good carbon, or brown, source.

*Citrus has somehow been saddled with a bad reputation as far as being used in compost piles. This reputation is undeserved. It's true that citrus peels such as oranges or grapefruit are stubborn about breaking down and therefore have the potential to cause less-than-fresh odors or possibly attract critters. Really, all they need is just a little push.

Citrus peels need to be chopped up and mixed well with materials that break down easily in a pile such as other kitchen scraps or grass or soft weeds. Other really tough decomposers are corn cobs and husks. These usually need to be run through a shredder to really break them up.

There is some wisdom, however, in not overwhelming a compost pile with massive amounts of citrus due to its high acid levels. The peelings and discarded amounts from a typical household kitchen are perfectly fine.

Prickly Problem

Layering dried brown grass clippings and green grass clippings over each other is usually discouraged, as mixing the two usually ends up becoming a matted clump which restricts the circulation of oxygen and creates a slimy, stinky mess.

Digging Deeper

When does a carbon material act like a nitrogen material? When straw has been used as bedding in a rabbit's cage. The straw (carbon) is soaked with rabbit urine and poop (nitrogen), which changes the original properties quite a bit. Now this carbon product acts more like a nitrogen product for your compost pile. This is a prime example of why it's futile to do math while composting.

Water Works

Every living thing needs water to survive, and your compost critters are no exception; you don't want to deprive them of this basic need. Your goal is to have the organic materials in your pile decompose as quickly as possible, and one of the best ways to guarantee this happening is to have nearly equal amounts of water and air in the pile. The ideal compost pile will have about 40 percent moisture in it. When the moisture level goes down, the decomposition slows because the microbes can't function effectively in a dry pile.

If the moisture content rises above 60 percent, your pile will become air deficient. This places a welcome mat at the front door for *anaerobic* bacteria to move on into the pile. Whether you're building a hot or cold pile, you do want to keep it as *aerobic* as possible.

def•i•ni•tion

Anaerobic is living or active in the absence of free oxygen. Anaerobic bacterial organisms are those that occur when oxygen is absent in a compost pile.

Aerobic is living or occurring only in the presence of oxygen. An aerobic compost hosts aerobes, or bacterial organisms that thrive in an oxygen-rich environment. Aerobes are the most effective of the decomposing bacteria. Thus, an aerobic compost pile is said to be an "active" pile.

Situating your pile near a water spigot or any other reliable water source will help your efforts to maintain moisture. Is your pile or bin in full sun, part shade, or somewhere in between? Location also dictates how often you'll need to add moisture.

Some people believe that chlorinated water can cause some casualties within the microcommunity of your pile, but I don't personally know anyone who has any problem with using chlorinated tap water.

Wise Worm

If you have a hot compost pile, you'll want to be careful about sticking your hand directly into the center due to possible high temperatures. Also, pull on some rubber or gardening gloves if you don't like the idea of touching decomposing material.

If you're interested in 100 percent chemical-free compost, you'll want to use rainwater from a rain barrel or well water to avoid adding unwanted chemicals in city water supplies. Some people deactivate the chlorine in regular tap water by placing it in an open container for a day or two and letting it sit out in the elements.

The rule of thumb here—and I love rules of thumb—is to keep your heap about as moist as a wrung-out sponge. You can perform another nonscientific test by sticking your hand into the pile, and pulling out a handful of compost from close to the middle. Give the handful a good squeeze. If a drop or two of water drips off, it's looking pretty good. But I'd aim for one drop or less. Of course, the outer edges of the pile will be on the drier side, but that's what turning is for.

A Breath of Fresh Air

Air should be one of your first considerations while you're building your compost pile. Aerobic bacteria are the hardest working bacteria in compost, but you'll only get them if your pile has a sufficient supply of oxygen. When there's little to no air in a pile, the aerobes die and their greedy cousins, the anaerobes, take over.

To be fair, anaerobic bacteria will break down organic materials eventually. But when it comes to speed and efficiency, the aerobes are far more effective. While the aerobes in an active pile are performing post-haste, they generate a lot of energy.

This energy aids not only in decomposition, but in the reproduction of yet more aerobes! As a bonus, the aerobes give off phosphorus, nitrogen, magnesium, and a host of other valuable nutrients for plants. All of this is conveniently dumped directly into your compost.

Another good reason to invite aerobes to the party is, quite frankly, the smell. When the anaerobes move in, they bring their own stinky baggage. When anaerobic material gets to work, it tends to leave behind hydrogen sulfide. If you're not sure what this smells like, recall the scent of rotten eggs.

Putrescine and cadaverine are two more end products of anaerobic activity. If you look closely at those two words, you may be able to surmise that they can't possibly smell any better than rotten eggs.

Even if you choose to build a passive pile, you should at least understand why things are moving slower—as much as 90 percent slower—than an active pile. After all, there are some sound reasons for choosing a cold pile and we'll talk more about that later. Even with a slow-moving pile, you can still put things in place that allow oxygen to be introduced even if you don't ever once turn the heap over.

Digging Deeper

In the interest of oxygen, size matters. If your compost pile is too large, it can interfere with aeration. Aim for a height and width of 5 to 6 feet and as long as your heart desires. You'll need at least 3 feet all the way around to get any decent heat in there.

A Little Help from Your Friends: Activators and Inoculators

If you've done any research on composting, you've probably heard about compost activators and inoculators. These are things you can purchase to add to your compost pile to speed up the decomposition process. Some activators can even be found around the house.

Activators are primarily a loaded nitrogen source used to heat up the pile. Inoculators (or microbial activators) are usually a source of microorganisms that you can add instead of waiting for these decomposers to arrive by themselves. There are a couple of schools of thought on why people use activators in their compost piles.

First of all, let me assure you that you do not need to run to the store and buy activators and/or inoculators. Your pile will manage the decomposition process just fine without them, thank you very much. However, if you're in a hurry, activators and inoculators can certainly speed the process along.

Simply by creating your pile on bare ground will bring in all the microbes necessary for great compost. Mother Nature is so far ahead of us in this game that we're usually left spinning our wheels trying to outsmart her. The same goes for the carbon/nitrogen balance in the pile. Using the browns and greens around our homes will work just fine.

That said, there are times when adding an activator or inoculator can be helpful. By all means, give it a go and try some of the following compost boosters; it couldn't hurt, and I find your dedication commendable:

- **Mineral rock powders such as lime, sulfur, gypsum, crushed oyster shell, and rock phosphate.** These minerals will work to get a pile going but won't necessarily keep the pile heated up. They may be better off being used as a soil amendment.

- **Biodynamic activators are plant-based materials and include chamomile, dandelion, yarrow, nettle, and valerian.** While these have proven to be effective activators, they aren't as widely used as some others.

- **Microbial activators are the fungi and bacteria more commonly called inoculators.** They typically come in a box as a dry powder, which you activate by mixing with water. These are great for pouring onto a newly constructed compost pile. However, if the bottom of your pile is touching the ground, you'll usually get all the microbial activity you'll need from the ground, and so these activators are unnecessary. My favorite way to add microbes to a new pile is to spread some compost from a previous pile onto it.

♦ **Nutritional activators are the ones you may have on hand around your house.** Plant meals high in protein, such as alfalfa pellets (rabbit food) and chicken feed, can be used as activators. Other common household activators are lime; blood meal; poultry, rabbit, and horse manure; or dry dog food.

Artificial Activators

While there are many ways to go about activating or inoculating your compost, the organic activators are going to be your best bet. Artificial activators—in the form of chemical fertilizers—are also on the market, but in the final analysis they aren't especially effective. The fertilizers lack the protein we find in organic products like animal manure (herbivores) and some vegetable matter.

The other problem with using chemical fertilizers, such as ammonium sulfate, is that it's easier to overdo the nitrogen. If you go all Rambo with the nitrogen, it could begin to take on a strong ammonia smell. It also goes to waste—the nitrogen just breaks down and then disappears.

Prickly Problem

Ammonium sulfate has been shown to cause harm to earthworms, so I urge you to avoid it as an activator in your compost. Redworms and night crawlers are extremely important to healthy soil. Some people spread ammonium sulfate on their lawns as a temporary super-green booster. Try grasscycling for the same brilliant green effect. It's effective, cheap, and kind to living organisms.

Organic Commercial Activators and Inoculators

Commercial organic activators are sold in a bag or box. They usually contain nitrogen, phosphorus, potassium, and microorganisms.

Some inoculators are sold as dissolvable tablets consisting of dormant bacteria and fungi. Herbal inoculators may include comfrey, dandelion, valerian, chamomile, and nettle. Companies claim that these products not only speed up the decomposition process but enhance the nutritional qualities of finished compost.

On-Hand Organic Activators

If you're curious and would like to give applied activation a try, go for something that you may have on hand instead of coughing up the bucks for it. Simple organic activators you may have on hand are lime (limestone); blood meal (yes, it's actually dried blood); and poultry, rabbit, and horse manure. Rabbit food (pellets) and dry dog food are also organic activators that people often have on-hand.

Traditionally, bone meal has been used as an activator; however, since the Mad Cow disease outbreak in Britain a while back, some people have stopped using it. While authorities claim that contracting Mad Cow from bone meal is improbable, if you have any concern at all, try using fish bone meal in its place.

A most interesting free compost activator is human urine. Human urine is punched up with nitrogen, minerals, and vitamins, making it a dandy activator. Of course, there's always the quickest and easiest way to activate a new compost pile: take a coffee can full of previously made compost and toss it into a new pile.

The Ratio Run-Around: Why You're Not Going to Need Math

The ratios (math) are the part of composting that makes people a little crazy. Every time I see someone explaining it to a new gardener-would-be-composter, it makes me a little crazy, too. I watch as their eyes glaze over and a small part of their brain shuts down. So I'm going to make you a promise and then tell you a secret.

While I feel obligated to explain the carbon-to-nitrogen (C:N) ratios (because it's actually kind of cool to know), this is the first and last time you'll hear me get into specific ratios, okay? Composting isn't brain surgery, and no one is going to lose an eye or take away your birthday if the ingredients aren't precise.

Now here's a secret: compost happens.

Get what I'm saying? If you rake organic matter into a pile then walk away, never to return, you're eventually going to have compost. I know—it's a miracle.

Here's the ratio run-around. Every living thing on Earth has a carbon-to-nitrogen value. When we're composting, the idea is to attempt to put the two amounts together in a way that makes decomposition happen effectively. The only reason people talk about the C:N ratio is because, well, they are impatient. People typically want the black gold that is humus as fast as they can get their grubby little hands on it. Otherwise, specific ratios don't matter one bit. Compost happens.

The C:N ratio gives us a reference point from which to begin (and continue) to mix and balance the ratios in our compost. This is not about figuring out the carbon-to-nitrogen balance in the compost every morning. Far from it!

For now, let's assume you'd like to get some nutrient-rich compost as fast as you can. It's the beginning of May and you have a new veggie bed, so you're just chompin' at the bit to get some of the good stuff into the new garden before you plant. You've started a compost pile, and you're looking to get things heated up in there. The only problem is that it doesn't seem to be doing much of anything.

Just looking at that pile will give you clues as to what you'll need to add in order to coax it into decomposing faster. You tossed dry leaves in there, some wood shavings, and a few pieces of cardboard. After that, you pulled quite a few weeds and tossed them in there, too. You've been keeping the pile damp, but not soaked. So you've done a lot of things right.

But the fact that you have mostly brown materials in there tells you that your pile, for the most part, is all about carbon. You gave it just a little tease with the nitrogen in the form of the weeds. The pile will eventually decompose, but to speed things up, you'll need to toss more green (seedless) weeds or grass clippings in there. You could also add rabbit or chicken manure. Your original pile may have had a C:N ratio of about 80:1, whereas an optimal pile is in the neighborhood of 30:1.

The exact ratio doesn't matter. Instead, use this formula: strive for 1 part carbon to 1 part nitrogen, 1 brown to 1 green, or 50/50. This is the way I've always done it, it's the way our local Master Gardeners teach it, and it works beautifully. After that, I keep an eye on the pile to see what it's telling me. If there's too little going on, I add some nitrogen-rich goodies. If the pile is too full of wet, green-type stuff, I throw in some carbon. Composting is as much an art as it is science. My compost heaps are always steaming when I turn them over and I never, *ever* do math.

Digging Deeper

Skip the math. An easy rule of thumb is to put half carbon (brown stuff) and half nitrogen (green stuff) into your compost pile to begin with. Then let the pile tell you what to toss in next. Whatever you do, don't stress over it; compost happens.

The Least You Need to Know

- Microbial bacteria are the invisible workhorses of decomposition in a compost pile.

- Macrobial decomposers are the visible critters that break down larger material, exposing more surface area for the microbes to finish the work.

- There's no such thing as too much air in a compost pile.

- Compost piles need to be kept as moist as a wrung-out sponge.

- There's no need to brush up on your math skills to create a compost pile. Use the 50/50 formula.

- Composting is as much about art as it is about math. Don't worry, compost happens!

Gathering the Goods

In This Chapter

- Kitchen scraps
- Animal manures
- Stuff to avoid
- Thick woody stuff
- pH basics

The previous chapter gave a basic overview of the types of materials that make up a good compost pile. This chapter offers more specific advice on what should and should not be thrown onto the pile—covering everything from kitchen scraps, manure, and weeds to thick woody stems and old newspapers.

Of course, some stuff is better left out of your compost pile because it is just plain bad for plants and/or people. You'll also learn about your composting options for thick, woody stems that come from tree and shrub prunings. And finally, there's a little ditty on soil pH and some talk on why paper is the answer to many composting problems.

The Best Place for Kitchen Waste

Among the greens and browns that you'll need for building a proper compost are those waste materials found in your kitchen. The majority of the common food-type kitchen waste is green material, but not everything. There are even some things, like eggshells, that are pH neutral.

Kitchen scraps that get the green light for your compost pile include fruit peelings, vegetable trimmings, grains, cereals, eggshells, coffee grounds (filters, too), tea bags, and the like. For composting purposes, kitchen scraps do not include dairy, meat, fish, fat products, or oil.

While these last things end up breaking down eventually (after all, they *are* organic materials), they also tend to create nasty odors that attract wildlife. Nothing says "Dinner!" to raccoons or skunks like rotting meat, fat, or dairy stuff.

Even veggie scraps can encourage curious raccoons to shop the produce aisle in your compost pile. Because most wildlife can't manage the secure lids on container-type compost bins, they're one of the best places to toss kitchen scraps. Use open-type compost piles for compostable items that don't attract wildlife the way food scraps do.

Another way to compost with kitchen scraps is to use them in a technique called "trench composting," which we'll talk about in Chapter 4. There's also my favorite place for kitchen goods: the worm bin, which we'll get into in Part 2.

If the wild critters around your place are larger than a respectable bread box, you can always opt to purchase a completely contained bin that has a locking door. After just a few weeks of composting, every gardener develops his own system that works best for his lifestyle. Personally, open compost bins work the best for my situation, so I feed my kitchen scraps to my worms in their condo or I stash them in a small, secured commercial composter.

Kitchen Compost Crock, Pail, or Bucket

As I've noted previously, composting should be *convenient* and *easy*. The more convenient you make things for you and your family to compost your scraps, the more likely you'll be to do it. That's why it's a good idea to keep a scrap container in your kitchen that stores your peelings and other kitchen scraps until you're ready to add them to the compost pile. Whether it's an old coffee can, a ceramic crock, or a decorative metal bin, as long as it has a lid and holds your waste, you're good to go.

I gather my food stuffs in my disposable plastic tub for a couple of days then split it between my worms and the contained compost bin. (Although, I do have the picture of a lovely kitchen compost crock stapled to my birthday list ....)

Wise Worm

Many coffeehouses such as Starbucks bag up their used coffee grounds and give them away! Some gardeners spread the grounds around their azaleas and other acid-loving plants, but I toss them into my compost piles and worm bins.

Good Animal Manures

Certain animal manures are the best gifts you can give to your compost. First off, they are wonderfully high in nitrogen. As manures break down, they build soil structure, porosity, stability, and hold nutrients beneficial to plants, as well as micro and macro compost critters. However, when it comes to manure, there's an important distinction between waste produced by herbivores exclusively (or nearly exclusively) and waste produced by meat-eating animals such as dogs or cats.

Manure commonly used for compost piles come from horses, cows, rabbits, llamas, alpacas, sheep, and goats. Other excellent manure sources come from animals that not only eat plants but may add a little protein to their diets. These animals include chickens, ducks, geese, pigs, and bats (guano).

Rabbit manure is my hands-down favorite manure for compost piles. For many people, rabbit manure is easier to come by than horse manure. Another nice thing about rabbit manure is that worms adore it; they tend to flock, er, squirm, to any site that has even a hint of bunny poop.

Manure from herbivores such as cows or horses is called "hot manure." Seasoned composters will tell you that when hot manures are applied fresh to a compost pile they create such a heated uproar within the pile that some decomposers may be killed. Usually, the carnage is minimal and the composters I know go ahead and toss the hot manures onto their piles without letting them dry out first.

Gardeners have voiced their concern over weed seeds in manure being added to their gardens. While there's some merit to the concern, my personal thoughts are that the value manure has for my plants far outweighs a couple of weeds I *may* have to pull later. Not to mention, if you keep an active or hot compost pile—as opposed to cold compost pile—most of the weed seeds that are brought in from any material should end up being killed off by the heat.

Some food for thought if you become the happy recipient of horse manure: usually horses are dewormed on a regular basis, and the manure gathered could possibly have traces of dewormer in it. Not such good news for the earthworms and red worms that would like to hang around and help decompose your compost pile.

Furthermore, in some parts of the country there have been reports of gardens being contaminated by the herbicides in the manure that has been taken from large cattle operations. The herbicides ended up killing the plants. So it makes sense to ask some questions of your manure source.

Who We're Not Inviting to the Party

Some material is best left out of your compost pile even though it may be technically biodegradable. Some of these products contain pathogens that threaten human health, some may attract undesirable wildlife, and some may create an unhealthy situation for plants.

Manures produced by carnivorous animals (meat-eaters) are in a different—lower—class than the herbivorous manures. Not only does dog and cat waste smell like an outhouse while it's rotting, it also attracts unwanted wildlife such as rats, skunks, and raccoons.

Probably the most compelling reason you want to dispose of meat-eating animal waste in a proper receptacle is because these manures may carry pathogens and parasites that are harmful to humans. I should mention that there are some people who have constructed ways to compost their dog and cat waste with a separate carnivore-poop-type method. But these materials have no business in your home composting bin, and meat-composting methods go beyond the scope of this book.

> **Prickly Problem** _____
>
> Although cat litter is technically biodegradable, it isn't something you should toss into the compost heap. Even if the cat waste is removed, it's possible for the litter to be contaminated with the nematode *Toxocra cati*, which can cause infections in the eyes as well as other organs, and the parasite *Toxoplasma gondii*, which can cause brain and eye disease in fetuses.

Dairy products are a no-no for the compost pile because rotting milk will put you off nearly as fast as rotting meat. Milk products can also cause pest problems.

Fat and grease should be disposed of properly and placed into a tightly sealed container called a tallow bin. The bin then needs to be taken to your local hazardous waste facility. Otherwise, place it in any other leak-proof container and into a waste receptacle. Adding fat and grease into a compost bin is the same as adding meat.

Pest poisons such as pesticides and insecticides should never be used in compost piles. These toxic chemicals will not only kill off the beneficial micro- and macroorganisms inside the compost pile, but you don't want chemical-laden compost added to your vegetable or flower beds, either.

Coal ashes contain large amounts of sulfur, as well as heavy metals such as iron and arsenic. This stuff is flat-out toxic to plants. Don't even think about it.

Nonbiodegradable stuff such as disposable baby diapers, rubber, plastic, glass, aluminum, and synthetic materials.

> **Prickly Problem** _____
>
> Leave animal bones such as chicken and beef out of your compost pile. Not only will they attract unwanted wildlife, but they can get brittle or sharp and cause injury to the gardener. Bones take a tremendous amount of time to decompose and won't be of any use in the near future, anyway.

Diseased plants should be thrown into the yard waste receptacle rather than your compost pile because, while the actual plant decomposes, very often the diseases do not. In fact, if the compost isn't heated up to ideal temperatures (and on occasion even that doesn't work) the diseases hang around and may multiply. You don't want to put that back into your garden beds.

Garden soil, whether from the yard or purchased, isn't necessary to add to a compost pile. While it isn't harmful in any way, soil adds little (if any) benefits to the composting process. Plus, it just makes the pile harder to turn over.

Paper: The Forgotten Carbon

Beginning compost builders are often concerned that they won't have enough browns on hand to build an active or even sufficient compost pile. The answer is paper—all types of it. While paper holds little in the way of valuable nutrients, it's a great equalizer by using up a huge amount of nitrogen as it breaks down. The typical family has more paper lying around than they think. Paper can come in the form of writing paper, wrapping paper, bills, junk mail, and shredded documents.

Paper can also take the shape of cardboard egg cartons and toilet paper rolls. One paper product that's plentiful in most homes is newspaper. The old school of thought was that the ink in newspaper carried heavy metals; not so in today's world. Newspapers today use vegetable dyes and other nontoxic materials for their printing ink.

Digging Deeper

Because too much cardboard can be overwhelming to a home-composting system, the best place for large amounts of thick or heavy cardboard may be in a traditional recycling container, as a weed barrier in the garden, or as a mulch in paths or walkways.

When composting paper, you want to be careful not to simply place layer after layer on top of each other. This will make the paper too thick and you'll have to then counteract the heavy carbon material with a major nitrogen material. Paper should be mixed thinly into the pile or, better yet, run through a paper shredder first.

What to Do with Fat Woody Waste

What about woody waste materials, such as prunings from shrubs, woody perennials, and trees?

The first thing I do is separate the wood by general thickness (remember, I don't think too hard about any of this stuff—I have a life). Every piece that's thicker than a pencil I place into a pile of its own. The pieces that are pencil-thick or thinner, I toss into one of my compost piles. Now you're left with what I call the "fat" woody waste.

These big boys are high in carbon and don't have much in the way of surface area for the microbial and macrobial critters to work with right away. Before you tie it up and haul it out for the garbage disposal service to pick up, consider some other options.

Here's where you get the last laugh on that person at your Bunko group who snickered behind your back when your husband gave you that chipper for Valentine's Day. A shredder/chipper is the best way of creating more surface area so the branches can decompose quickly with your other materials in the pile.

When you place the branches in the chipper, you want to have the materials finely chopped if you're adding it to compost. If you didn't receive a chipper for Valentine's Day, it belongs at the top of your Christmas list. Or make it a "gift" for your husband or wife. Keep reading for useful and creative ways to use fat woody waste in your yard or garden.

Making Mulch

Another way to use branches in the chipper is to run the wood through the chipper set on a "coarse" chipping setting. This breaks the woody stuff into smaller pieces, but leaves them big enough to act as a mulch in your flower beds. The mulch will keep the moisture in the soil and help suppress weeds.

Wonderful Wildlife Habitat

You may have a backyard wildlife habitat in your yard or perhaps you just like the idea of lending a helping hand to animals. Little mammals, insects, and invertebrates depend upon places like dead branches and tree snags for shelter and raising their young. Nothing makes great shelter for wildlife like a big pile of fat woody waste. Large logs blended with medium and smaller fat woody waste are perfect for this type of project.

Its Own Space

As I've mentioned several times already, compost happens. It's just a matter of *when* it happens. Fat woody waste will eventually break down, so if you have the space, why not make a neatly stacked pile far off in a corner somewhere and give it its own space to decompose the way nature intended—very slowly.

Heat

If you have a fireplace or wood stove or even an outdoor fire pit, you can cut up large logs to burn. You can then compost the resulting wood ash, although I wouldn't use bucket after bucket of wood ash in a compost pile as it can raise the pH levels of the pile, possibly making the soil too alkaline.

 Wise Worm

Did you know there are companies that charge people to haul away their yard and farm manure? These companies compost the materials and sell it back to the public as compost for their gardens!

A Word About pH

There's no point in getting tripped up by soil pH any more than doing the nitrogen-to-carbon math. Yes, you can test soil and, yes, some plants like their pH a little higher or lower than others. But when the curtain goes up, you're going to have fairly neutral soil due to all the great compost you're adding, anyway.

Scientists have devised a pH number line that represents the range between alkaline and acidic. Soils fall somewhere on that line between 1 to 14. At 1.0, the soil is at the highest level of acidity or the most "sour." At 14.0 it is the highest in alkaline or the most "sweet." The neutral place on the pH line is 7.0. Most plants are thrilled to be living in soils that are anywhere from 6.0 to 7.5—a little on the sweet side. Some plants, such as azaleas and camellias, do prefer their soil a little acidic.

Here's where the beauty of composting comes in. Compost is a wonderful pH buffer. That is, it brings the soil to close to neutral while providing easily accessible nutrition to plants' roots, which makes the plant less and less dependent on the pH levels of the soil.

If there's a certain area of your yard with acid lovers such as camellias, rhododendrons, and azaleas, make a special batch of compost for that bed. Add acidic materials, such as pine needles, citrus, sawdust, and oak leaves, to the decomposing compost. Conversely, if you'd like to sweeten your soil, add wood ash or lime to your compost pile to raise alkaline levels.

If you want to test your soil's pH level out of curiosity, control freakiness, or because you're adding some new plants and would like to see if you're giving them a happy home, by all means do so! It's interesting to see just what the ground beneath your feet has to offer. Home soil test kits are available at local garden centers or online catalogs. These tests are easy to perform, but they aren't as accurate as tests performed by your state's university extension office or private testing facilities.

Often when composting gardeners test their soils, they go ahead and test their compost piles, as well. A word of warning about testing compost: while compost piles are in the process of decomposing organic matter, they all go through fluctuating pH cycles. Newer piles tend to be acidic and continue to slide up and down the pH bar during the process. If you give your compost pile enough oxygen, the finished product will have neutralized on its own and fall into the 6.5 to 7.0 range.

Personally, I don't test my compost piles, but I do add tons of variety to them while they're cooking. My inner control freak is surpassed only by my inner laziness. The key here is not to overthink anything about this process to the point where you give up on the whole idea of composting. It really isn't going to make or break your compost one way or the other. Do your best to add a variety of organic materials into the mix and forget about it. Compost happens, and all compost is awesome.

The Least You Need to Know

- The best place for kitchen scraps is in a rodent- and critter-resistant composting bin or a worm bin.

- Good animal manures to use in compost piles are those manures that come from herbivores or nearly herbivores such as chickens.

- Don't forget about everyday household paper as a carbon material.

- Fat woody waste can be run through a chipper, or it can be used as a mulch, as a wildlife habitat, in the fireplace, or in its own compost pile.

- Don't overthink pH. Add a variety of materials to your pile as you're building it and let Mother Nature handle the rest.

Chapter 4

Some Like It Hot, Some Like It Cold

In This Chapter

- ◆ Hot composting versus cold composting
- ◆ How to build a hot compost pile
- ◆ How to build a cold compost pile
- ◆ Simple trench composting

Composting can be as easy or as labor-intensive as you'd like it to be. If you balance your greens and browns and turn your pile regularly, you're going to have compost or humus very quickly. But if you'd rather just throw a bunch of scraps and yard waste willy-nilly into a pile and not give it another thought, you're also going to end up with compost … just not as quickly.

What it comes down to is this: there are good reasons to create a hot (fast) compost pile, and there are just as many reasons to go with a cold (slow) one. This chapter will help you figure out which type is going to work best for you and your lifestyle.

The Advantages and Disadvantages of Heating Things Up

Hot composting is also referred to as "fast" composting. The primary advantage of hot composting is, of course, speed. Gardeners want their humus as fast as naturally possible. Another advantage of fast piles is that the heat generated in the pile can kill undesirable pathogens that lurk within the materials as well as burn up any weed seeds.

Because fast piles break down quickly, the nutrients don't leach out of the compost, and the final product tends to hang on to the good stuff better than compost created via the cold process. The speed of a hot pile allows decomposition to happen so quickly that flies and other pests are less likely to move in.

Hot composting can produce usable humus in as fast as 3 to 4 weeks. The biggest drawback to fast composting is that there's a fair amount of work involved. For one thing, you're going to need to pay a little more attention to making sure you're adding a good balance of greens and browns to heat up the process.

Then there's the biggie—turning the pile. For some people, this isn't a bother at all. For others, not only does it sound like too much work but they're just hoping to remember the pile is out there.

Another concern with a hot pile is that while harmful bacteria that causes disease are killed, so is the good bacteria—good bacteria and fungi that would otherwise hang around in the finished compost to help plants fight off future pathogens that attack plants as they're growing.

Keys to Building a Hot Compost Pile

The ideal temperature range for a hot pile is between 113°F and 160°F at the pile's core. Compost thermometers, which work like a meat thermometer, will give you an accurate reading of just how hot it's getting in there, but it's not necessary to run out and purchase one. When I turn my piles and see steam rising from inside, I know the decomposers are working their magic.

Usually, I can't resist sticking my hand into the pile and grabbing some material from the middle. I'm almost always rewarded with a handful of soil that smells like fresh earth. If this describes your compost pile, you'll likely be harvesting the first batch in about eight weeks. But in order to achieve this level of gardening nirvana, you'll want to abide by the following guidelines:

Put it in contact with the ground. No matter what kind of compost pile you decide to build, it's best to start it on bare ground. You can construct whatever type of container you'd like to confine the organic materials you've gathered—but let the bottom of the pile come in contact with the earth. When the materials touch the ground, the micro- and macroorganisms that are naturally present in the soil are quickly drawn to the pile; once they move in, they'll help make the transition from waste to humus even faster.

Digging Deeper

What about the good bugs and worms? Will a hot pile burn them up? Don't worry about the macroorganisms; they'll simply migrate to the outer limits until things cool down again.

Do it all at once. Most hot compost piles are built "all at once." That is, you add all of the brown and green ingredients at the same time and don't add more later. Although it is not absolutely necessary, doing so ensures that the materials break down at roughly the same time so that you don't end up with "half-baked" stragglers.

Size matters. To achieve any heat at all, your pile will need to be at least 3' wide × 3' tall and deep, but it's more ideal at 4' × 6' wide, tall, and deep. Any taller or thicker than that and the pile could become anaerobic. You can make the pile as long as you'd like, as long as you keep it between 3 and 6 feet tall and thick.

Aerate it. Air reaches into a pile from all sides to about 1 to 2 feet deep, but after that, you'll have to help out by either turning the pile a few times a week or adding ventilation stacks (see Chapter 5). Good aeration allows the center of the compost pile to heat up, and the organic materials begin to break down.

Frequent aeration is one of the biggest factors in a hot pile. Turning it a couple of times a week is sufficient. Don't turn it any more than that or the bacteria won't have a chance to decompose the materials.

Keep it moist ... but not too moist. The pile must also have sufficient moisture in order to invite the microbes in to begin the decomposition process. As mentioned in Chapter 2, a good rule of thumb is to keep the pile about as damp as a wrung-out sponge.

Add water to the pile as necessary because if the pile is allowed to dry out, the process slows to a crawl—which is the opposite of hot composting. On the other hand, if the pile is sopping wet it'll become oxygen-depleted, and this is also the opposite of hot composting, but smells worse.

Reserve a little "starter" compost for the next pile. After you've spread the first batch in your vegetable garden, perennial bed, or foundation planting, start a new pile in the same place. The leftover compost from the previous batch will act as an activator to jump-start the new pile. The next heap could be ready to go even faster than the last.

Wise Worm _____

Even though all organic materials break down eventually, the smaller those organic material pieces are, the easier it is for organisms to decompose them. Keep layers of yard clippings to 6 inches or less. Limiting the size will mean the difference between harvesting compost in weeks as opposed to months.

The Advantages and Disadvantages of Just Chillin'

Cold compost piles work at temperatures 90 degrees and below. At these cooler temperatures it takes longer—between 6 months to a year or more—to harvest compost. Some gardeners will tell you that cold composting is inferior to hot compost piles. These gardeners would go on to say that cold piles aren't desirable. I don't buy it. Cold composting is simply a different way of ending up with the same valuable product, and there are terrific reasons for opting for a passive pile.

The biggest advantage of a slow or passive compost pile is that it's easy to start, add to, and maintain. Actually, easy doesn't begin to describe it, because there's literally zero work after you toss organic matter into a pile or bin. People with busy lives are partial to this type of composting.

Then there are those people who don't produce much in organic matter and would have a difficult time finding enough materials to start a nice-sized hot pile.

And let's face it, some folks without Type-A personalities may simply not be in any hurry.

Another advantage to the passive pile is that the humus created in it is better at suppressing soilborne diseases because, unlike the hot pile, the fungi and bacteria that destroy these diseases aren't killed off by the high temperatures. The downside is that this type of pile could take a year or more to be considered usable compost for the garden. Of course, if it's in a hidden corner of the yard and you're in no hurry, this won't make a difference.

What *could* make a difference to you is that these cold piles are at risk for not getting enough oxygen and possibly becoming smelly. You may also notice that some of the scraps and yard waste you tossed into the pile might actually start growing before they break down. While this isn't going to ruin the compost, there are some materials you may want to avoid putting into a cold pile. Things such as weeds that have seeds on them and *any* piece of potato. Potatoes seem to be able to spring up out of the smallest chunks.

There is a certain freedom in creating a passive compost pile. By freedom I mean you can do pretty much whatever you'd like with it. Ideally, you still want to get both browns and greens in there, and some manure if you can swing it. You pile the materials into whatever bin you choose—or just create an open pile way off in a secluded area of your yard or property—and watch it rot. On second thought, you don't have the time to stay and watch. Just add to the pile whenever you have some great materials and let nature do the rest.

The Hybrid Pile

My favorite composting method is a hybrid between the hot and cold compost technique—a warm pile, if you will. For me, this is a happy medium. I basically build it as if I were making a hot pile originally, but once it's thrown together I give it less attention than a hot pile requires.

For instance, I only turn it once every couple of weeks, and I don't worry so much about the moisture and temperature levels. There's no real formula here, but with the warm method I get compost in a decent amount of time, and it's odor-free because I give it a little love every once in a while. With the hybrid method, I have great compost ready to spread in about eight weeks.

Trench Composting

Trench or pit composting is cold composting at its simplest. The concept is as elementary as it comes. You dig a trench or hole between 1 and 2 feet deep anywhere in your yard or garden, toss organic waste inside the trench or pit, cover it up, and then forget about it.

There's no bin to make or purchase and no need to think about the right balance of greens and browns. There's literally no turning, aerating, or wondering. Eventually, the organic materials will decompose and turn into compost, automatically adding nutrients to the nearby soil in your garden. And because the waste is buried in the ground, it actually stays warmer during the cold months and holds moisture longer during the warm months.

Farmers have been practicing a larger scale version of this technique for years. They dig deep underground furrows to hold large amounts of organic waste like hay and manure. As a backyard composter, you can use this style on a smaller scale.

The depth of the trench is determined by just how much organic material you want to bury. This type of simple pit composting becomes especially handy while you're puttering around your garden deadheading flowers or removing spent or fallen fruits and veggies because you no longer have to walk to and from the compost pile.

A variation on this theme is to dig a long trench right in front of your vegetables—one row at a time. Put your spent plants, ruined veggies, kitchen waste, and other compostable goodies in the trench and then cover it up. The resulting compost will act as a side dressing of nutrients for the plants.

Similarly, if you have footpaths between rows of vegetables, dig a trench right down the middle of the footpath. Bury the goods in the trench and then cover it back up with soil. Add a covering such as straw, grass clippings, cardboard, etc., for a firm footing so you can continue to use the path.

If you started the trenches in the early spring or beginning of summer, by next spring you should be able to uncover the trench and toss the new compost onto the garden bed where you'll be planting. In time, your entire garden bed will be transformed with excellent soil and nutrients.

Make a Compost Planter

If you have old hay or straw bales on hand that have become too moldy to feed to horses or cattle, use them as organic "planters" for pumpkins or other vegetables or flowers.

To create the planter, lay the hay bale so the cut edge is facing up and the baling twine is on the side. Using your hands, pry apart the straw until you have dug a couple of good-sized holes in the hay bale. Now, fill them with a mix of half compost and half soil. Thoroughly wet the bale with a hose and then plant either seeds or seedlings into the compost mixture. Many people use several bales and plant pumpkins so they can enjoy the vines crawling down them and because they make a great harvest scene for the fall.

Be sure to water the plants and bales thoroughly, as the straw dries out very quickly. After you've harvested the vegetables, usually the straw will be too broken down to replant. At this point you could add the rotting straw to a compost pile so it can finish decomposing. You could also start a new compost pile right there on the used straw bales. Just add a nitrogen source like grass clippings or manure. Build the compost pile as described earlier.

The Least You Need to Know

- ◆ Both hot and cold composting styles have their pros and cons.

- ◆ Hot composting involves the most work but it's the fastest way to get compost.

- ◆ Cold composting is slow but has the added benefit of nearly zero work.

- ◆ Trench composting is the simplest composting technique.

Containing Your Compost

In This Chapter

- How to make your own easy and cheap compost bins
- The pros of ready-made bins
- Where to put your bin

In this chapter, you'll find instructions for building many simple compost structures to house your garden gold while it's cooking. Plus, you'll get some tips for making your bin attractive and pull double-duty in the garden. And in case construction isn't your thing or you just can't wait to get started, you'll get the scoop on ready-made bins you can run out and purchase right away!

Do You Even Need a Bin?

Although you certainly can start and complete compost in a simple open pile on the ground, it's easier to heat up a contained pile.

Another reason to go with a bin is purely aesthetic. A compost bin of any sort looks nicer in your yard than an uncontained heap of garbage. If you live in close proximity to neighbors, containing your pile is simply the courteous thing to do.

The Cheap Seats: DIY Compost Bins

One of the perks of taking up composting is that the start-up costs are low. All you need is organic waste (free) plus some sort of container (as inexpensive as you want it to be).

Many do-it-yourself-type bins are incredibly easy to construct. But if you have two left thumbs, a wide variety of preconstructed bins are available at hardware stores, home improvement centers, and specialty garden suppliers.

Prickly Problem _____

If you build your own bin from wood or pallets, avoid using chemically treated lumber. The chemicals used to treat the wood are toxic and can leach into your compost. This is especially undesirable if you're planning to use the compost in your vegetable garden.

Wire Hoop Bin

Wire hoop bins are easy to set up, but it's a far easier task with two people. For this bin you'll need the following materials.

Materials:

   12½ feet of hardware cloth or horse fencing

   4 metal or plastic clips

   Four steel fence posts (also referred to as T-posts) or any other type of poles that can be hammered into the ground

Tools:

   Work gloves

   Goggles

   Heavy wire snips

   Pliers

   Metal file

   Hammer or post slammer

Instructions:

1. Roll out the wire. If you're using horse fencing, bend the wires that have the sharp end exposed back onto themselves with the pliers. If you're using hardware cloth, cut the wire at a cross wire so you don't end up with loose wires poking out. File down any sharp ends with the metal file.

2. Place the T-posts inside the hoop at evenly spaced intervals. Press the posts taut against the wire and pound them into the ground with a hammer or post slammer. Because hardware cloth is so strong, you may find you can forego the posts with this type of wire.

The specific size of the bin isn't important, but you'll want it to be *at least* 3' × 3' × 3'. By the way, your wire bin doesn't have to be a circle; it could end up as a square.

Hoop bin.

Three-Sided Picket-Fence Bin

Three-sided picket-fence bins are my favorite bins to build because they're easy to assemble and nice-looking. As an added bonus, their shape makes it easy to access and turn the compost. Begin by purchasing the following materials from a hardware or home improvement store.

Materials:

Two premade picket-fence panels

4 (3-inch) metal corner brackets

Box of 1" sheet rock screws (You could also use a hammer and nails instead of screws.)

Tools:

> Work gloves
>
> Goggles
>
> Screw gun or hammer
>
> Skill saw or hand saw

Instructions:

1. Cut the two panels in half to create four separate panels.

2. Secure three of the panels together by attaching the metal corner brackets to the 2 × 4s at the top and the bottom of the fence panels. One side of the pile will be open. You'll have one panel left over; save it to build another bin.

This bin literally takes under a half hour to build and is usually very inexpensive. If you ask around, you can probably score some or all of the materials for free.

You can also use wood pallets in place of the fencing. These are usually very easy to come by free of charge. If you build the bin so the pallet boards run horizontally along the top of the constructed bin, there'll be a space between the boards. This space is perfect for keeping garden forks, rakes, and shovels.

Picket-fence bin.

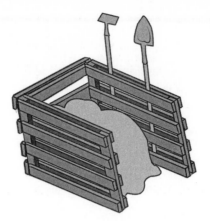

Pallet bin.

Cinderblock Bin

Although cinderblock bins appear more solid, they are just as easy to build as fence bins. You don't need to use mortar to secure the blocks, which can be dry-stacked 3 to 4 feet high and remain very stable. Build the walls so the blocks lie on the flat sides (so you can look through them) to create a built-in aeration system. A nice advantage to using cinderblocks is that they keep the compost pile warmer longer due to their passive solar capacity.

Cinderblock bin.

Garbage Can Bin

Garbage can bins are especially handy for those people short on space. They have a secure lid so you can throw your kitchen scraps inside without worrying about wildlife raiding the bin. To make the bin, you'll need an inexpensive, plastic garbage can and a drill.

Instructions:

1. Cut the bottom out of the can with a utility knife or saw.

2. Drill several 1-inch holes around the outside of the garbage can (opt for a few less in order to keep moisture in).

Wise Worm _____

It's fine to leave the can sitting on the level soil, but if you dig a trench 12" to 18" deep and the diameter of the can, you can place the can inside it and it will be less likely to blow over. The advantage of leaving the bottom of the can intact (with just a couple of air holes) is that you can roll the can around on its side every couple of days to get things heated up.

If you live in a climate where the contents of the can might freeze, you can provide some insulation for the bin by digging a hole 15" to 18" into the ground and sitting the can in it and placing straw bales around the garbage can.

Garbage can bin.

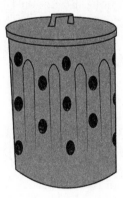

Used Tire Bin

If you have any old tires lying around, break them out and repurpose them as a compost container. You can use the tires just as they are; however, they're easier to work with if you remove the side walls with a sharp utility knife.

Instructions:

1. After you have your tires ready, place one on the bare earth and fill it with brown and green materials.

2. When that first tire is full, place another tire on top of the first and fill that one to the top.

3. Continue piling this way until you have five or six tires stacked and filled.

In a couple of weeks, remove the top tire and place it on the ground next to the first stack. Using a garden fork, transfer some of the contents from the original stack to the tire you just placed on the ground. Remove a second tire from the first pile, place it on the new stack, and transfer more material to it. Repeat the process until the original stack is completely moved to the second stack. Let a couple of weeks go by and repeat that procedure.

Tire bin.

Three-Unit Connected Bin

The concept behind a three-unit connected bin is that "turning" on your part is only done when the composting materials are moved from one bin to the next. Certainly, this doesn't stop you from turning the compost as many times as you'd like. But many gardeners use the first bin to gather all of their materials. When that bin is full, turn the materials into the next bin and start over with gathering new materials in the first bin again.

After a month, you turn the contents of the second bin into the third bin and let the compost finish from there. The third bin also acts as a holding area for finished compost until you need it. Personally, if I had room for the three-unit bin, I would turn the compost a couple of times while it was in the second (middle) bin in order to have my compost faster.

Most three-unit connected bins are constructed as one unit. If you're (or someone close to you is) handy with construction, this is a nice way to compost. The three-unit bin can be constructed in sections by using the three-sided picket-fence method or the cinderblock method.

Three-unit bin.

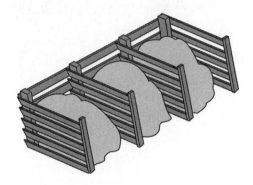

Store-Bought Bins

For people who aren't inclined to construct their own anything, another choice is to purchase a store-bought bin. You can find them in hardware stores as well as big-box stores such as Costco and Sam's Club. Store-bought bins are usually made of polypropylene, copolymer, or polymer, or even recycled plastics, but wood bins are also available. Most of the compost bins have no bottom so the materials rest on the bare soil, but some are completely enclosed. Almost all store-bought bins have a secure lid.

Because the most finished humus can be found at the bottom of the compost, some of these bins have little access doors at the bottom to make it easier to harvest the humus. On bins without doors, you'll need to lift the entire unit up and off of the compost so it can be gathered. Price-wise, the prefabricated compost bins are far more expensive than do-it-yourself bins. They range anywhere from $75 to $300.

Secure, store-bought bins are ideal for holding kitchen waste because they are animal-proof. Another nice thing about them is that the plastic is extremely good at absorbing the heat from the sun, so materials inside are quickly heated up, which means faster results.

Soil Saver store-bought bin.

(Courtesy of GoodCompost.com.)

Bins from Your Local Government

Many city or county governments sell prefabricated bins to residents. For instance, you might be able to purchase a bin that would normally cost $100 to $125 for $35—a substantial savings. Municipalities offer these discounts to encourage residents to send less garbage to the landfills.

Usually these bins do not have a bottom, leaving the material inside to rest on the bare soil. Many of these county bins are comprised of three or four removable sections, making it very easy to turn the composting materials.

After letting the full bin sit for a couple of weeks, you take the first section of the bin off the top and place it on the ground. Then, using the garden fork (or tool of choice), you take enough materials out of the bin to fill the first section. Next, you take the second section of the bin off and place it on top of the first section that you just filled, and continue the process until the sections are reassembled once again. You've now aerated the materials. Repeat this process as many times as you'd like.

County-supplied bins.

Tumbling Bins

Tumbling bins are always completely enclosed, like a barrel or a sphere, and are elevated on legs of some sort. They come in all shapes and sizes, but they can all be turned or spun to mix and aerate the compost. Because of the ease with which you can turn the contents, you are in a better position to get compost quickly. When composting in a tumbler, all the green and brown are added at one time. Also because they're not touching the open ground, they can't benefit from microorganisms that reside naturally in the soil to get things going. In this case you'll want to add a compost activator or inoculator. Tumbling bin prices range from $100 to $400.

Tumbleweed tumbling compost bin.

(Courtesy of GoodCompost.com.)

Digging Deeper _____

Do you have a winery in your area? Wine barrels eventually outlive their usefulness for holding grapes, and wineries often sell them for a steal. You can purchase one for about $40 to $50 and repurpose it as a tumbling compost bin.

Indoor Bins

Brand new to the composting scene are awesome little indoor composters that let you compost kitchen scraps right in your kitchen. These are especially ideal for apartment or condo dwellers who don't have the space for a normal-sized bin.

The small bin fits right inside a cabinet, laundry room, or garage and produces fresh compost in about two weeks. While indoor compost systems aren't cheap, they do increase your composting options. Indoor composters may be purchased for $250 to $350.

NatureMill indoor composting bin.

(Courtesy of NatureMill, Inc.)

A Few Words on Bin Location

If you have an open compost bin primarily made up of yard and garden clippings, it makes sense to place the pile in a far corner of your lot because you won't be visiting it daily. For household waste, placing the bin nearer to the house or kitchen door encourages family members to use it. Don't forget that what seems close on a beautiful summer morning will seem like a mile in the winter snow.

If you plan on using your compost in a new garden bed next spring, build the compost bin in that location at the end of the summer or early fall. When spring rolls around, you can remove the bin and the compost will be right where you need it, ready to spread.

Whether to situate your bin in a sunny or shady spot depends on your climate. If you live in California where winters are predominately mild (comparatively speaking), place your bin in the shade. The sun will deplete the compost pile of moisture. If you live in Minnesota and have freezing temperatures in the winter, go for a sunny spot.

> **Digging Deeper** _____
>
> You can make a homemade tumbling bin by recycling an empty 55-gallon plastic drum and adding organic waste to it. Drill a couple holes into the drum for aeration, but not too many, as you don't want the moisture evaporating quickly. Add your organic materials, then reseal the lid and roll it around every few days. You'll need to peek inside from time to time to be sure there's enough moisture.

I'll Take Two Bins, Please

As an avid gardener, I'm always looking for ways to gain as much soil as possible while also maximizing my time. I always have three types of bins going at one time. The first one is an active (hot) compost pile. I gather a balanced amount of browns and greens and fill up a bin (usually the three-sided open type). I stir things up and add some water to get things moving. I turn the pile a couple of times a week and, after about four to five weeks, I have compost on hand.

The second bin is a slower pile. I just add things from the yard or garden at random. I turn it when the mood strikes me, but I do make sure it stays moist so the pile doesn't slow to a pitiful crawl.

The third bin is my worm condo. I always have a worm bin in production for small amounts of kitchen waste, coffee, and tea grounds. Worm condos are covered in detail in Chapter 9.

Bins Can Be Beautiful

For some reason, no one has put pen to paper and figured out how to prefabricate a truly attractive compost bin. The good news is that when you build a bin yourself, you have complete creative license. Let me jump-start your imagination and give you some ideas.

Vines, Veggies, and Flowers

One of the easiest ways to make your compost bin a little easier on the eyes is to grow a vine crop on it. If you build a wood or wire bin, plant the seeds next to the outside of the bin and keep them watered. There's no end of ideas for this; you can plant beans, peas, cucumbers, and mini pumpkins. If you prefer just flowers, try sweet peas, morning glories, or pink jasmine.

If your compost structure has a solid edge along the top, you can mount flower boxes or place flowerpots on top. Plant whatever happens to be blooming. As far as handiness, don't forget that if you have (or are going to build) a compost bin using pallets, be sure to attach the pallets so that the outside boards run horizontally. This way you can use the spaces between the boards for garden forks, shovels, and even plant hangers.

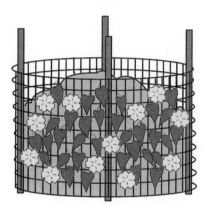

Compost bins can be beautiful.

Structural Beauty

A new paint job can do wonders for wood or cinderblock structures. You can paint fencing a classic white or a bold purple, and plant flowers at the base of the bin for an eye-catching focal point.

Keep your eyes open for attractive premade materials that can be used for a three-sided bin instead of picket fencing, wire, pallets, etc. I happened to spot some heavy plastic fencing that came in a variety of designs that would make a lovely bin. This would be perfect for a suburban setting—especially if you're trying to stay on friendly terms with neighbors who can see the bin from their front porch.

The Least You Need to Know

- ◆ Do-it-yourself bins are relatively inexpensive and easy to build.
- ◆ Commercial bins are excellent for kitchen waste and hiding piles.
- ◆ Where you locate your pile depends on what you put in it and where you'll be using the finished compost.
- ◆ Feel free to prettify your bins by planting vines around them, painting them, or using decorative materials.

Chapter 6

Zen and the Art of Compost Maintenance

In This Chapter

- Aerating and ventilating your pile
- Keeping your pile moist
- Compost troubleshooting
- Deterring unwanted wildlife
- Composting safely

Maintaining your compost pile is not complicated, physically difficult, or expensive. In fact, you'll find composting is one of the easiest hobbies you've ever picked up. But to keep your pile churning out garden gold on a regular basis, you need to do some basic compost maintenance. Once you have the bin and the goods to fill it with, it's time to start paying attention to the pile's air and moisture levels.

Aeration and Ventilation

In order for the microbial organisms to work their magic on your organic matter, they need oxygen. You can introduce fresh air into the compost pile in a number of ways.

Turning

The most common way to keep compost piles aerated involves turning the material in the pile using a garden fork or pitch fork. When you lift, turn, and mix the organic matter, you're automatically introducing air into the pile. You can also aerate the pile by physically moving it from one spot to another in layers. For compost piles contained in tumblers, it's a simple matter of turning the barrel a few times a week to mix up the contents.

A compost fork is a tool developed specifically for turning compost. It has five tines that are spaced wider than most traditional garden forks and has a long handle for good reach deep into the pile.

If you don't have a compost fork, you can use any long stick to poke holes into the pile. Even an old ski pole that's lost its mate can have a second life as a compost turner; the little basket at the end helps grab the materials.

My favorite tool for compost turning is the common garden fork. These forks are called different things by different people depending on the length of the handle and the number of tines (prongs). As long as you can maneuver the fork, use what works best for you. Sometimes I use the fork just to punch holes into the pile, too.

An assortment of aeration tools.

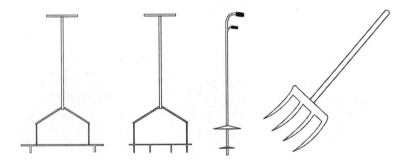

Wise Worm

Why pay top dollar for aeration tools—or any garden tools, for that matter? Ask friends and family if they have extras that need a home and keep an eye out for them at garage sales and flea markets. You can also join your local "freecycle.org" and watch craigslist (craigslist.org) for gently used tools.

If your pile has a fair amount of fibrous materials, turning it can become very difficult. If this is the case, you might give ventilation stacks a try.

Ventilation Stacks

You can introduce oxygen into parts of your pile that otherwise wouldn't get any by adding ventilation stacks. A ventilation stack is a huge plus to your pile and it's a very simple do-it-yourself trick. Ventilation stacks allow air to circulate through the middle of them. They could be fat PVC pipe with perforation holes or a simple bundle of sticks.

The key is to add the stacks early on—don't wait until you have a large pile to add the ventilation stack; by that time it'll become difficult to get a vent deep down inside the materials. Instead, install a vent in the center of the pile at the beginning of the compost building process. After that, just keep adding your browns and greens around it.

Bundled bamboo stakes or any other hollow posts secured together by twine, rope, or even plastic garden tape make great ventilation stacks. You can also use a perforated pipe (the kind laid under rocks for drainage), or even rolled up wire mesh.

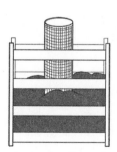  

Get creative with ventilation stacks for your compost pile.

Wise Worm _____

Another way of keeping your compost pile aerated is to use 3"-5" wood chips or wood brush as the bottom layer of your pile. These are coarse enough to allow air to circulate under and into the pile.

Build Air into Your Pile

A simple way of oxygenating your pile is to take coarse materials such as hedge trimmings or thick plant stalks (sunflower stalks are great for this) and layer them throughout the pile as it's being built. These materials are coarse enough to allow air to circulate throughout the pile. This works best for a cold pile that you won't be turning often because not only do fibrous materials take longer to break down, but they make the pile harder to turn.

Maintaining Moisture

Water is another essential ingredient for any high-efficiency compost pile. To get things started off right, spray some water in between the layers as you're building the pile. Don't add so much water that it puddles up or runs out of the bottom of the heap, though.

Digging Deeper _____

If you don't like the idea of sticking your hand—even a gloved one—into a pile to see if it feels like a wrung-out sponge, take a long stick and push it deep into the center. If the stick is damp when you pull it out, you're on the right track.

If you live in a hot climate, place your bin in a shady spot in your yard to keep it from drying out in the hot sun. In addition, cover any uncontained piles with plastic or cloth tarps, cardboard, burlap, or plywood to help maintain moisture.

Compost Troubleshooting

Nothing is perfect—compost included. The good news is that when your pile gets off track, there are usually obvious signs and simple solutions for steering it back in the right direction. And when it comes to compost, there isn't anything that can't be fixed. Even if you throw everything on the ground all willy-nilly, you will eventually end up creating garden gold.

The following sections highlight common compost problems and give you tips for setting things straight.

There's Nothing Going On in There

The problem: The pile hasn't changed in weeks.

The solution: Add water and/or green materials. To get the water throughout the pile you can turn it a section at a time, wetting the sections until they're damp. Then add more of your pile to this section and wet the stuff you put on top. Repeat this until it's a new—but damp—pile. If you don't want to (or can't) turn it, you can make deep holes in it and stick the garden hose inside to get it wet all the way through.

Don't forget to add some green (nitrogen) stuff; grass clippings would be ideal. Also add blood meal, or if you have a source for manure from an herbivore, it'll kick your pile into high gear.

It's Not Supposed to Smell, Right?

The problem: The pile smells bad.

The solution: First, you need to answer a few questions:

◆ Did you add the wrong food stuffs like meat, fish, dairy, eggs, or grease? If it's possible to remove these items, do so; otherwise, simply turn the smelly stuff into the pile and cover it with organic material.

◆ Did you add a thick pile of grass clippings the last time you mowed your lawn? If so, mix some carbon sources like leaves or newspaper into the wet grass clumps.

◆ Is the pile sitting in an area that gathers all the rain/water run-off? If your pile is a wet, soggy mess, then you have too much water or greens (nitrogen) in there. The first thing you need to do is aerate the pile by turning it, letting it get some oxygen. You probably need to add some browns (carbon), as well. Here's where newspaper, wood chips, or cardboard can save the day. And back off on adding water for a while.

If you notice that there are some anaerobic pockets, you simply mix them up and add browns. If the pockets seem past the point where you want to deal with them, you can remove them from the pile.

The Bad Weed Seed

The problem: You have a lot of weeds that you want to compost.

The solution: The issue of whether or not to add weeds to a compost pile comes up frequently. There's really no right or wrong answer. I can only tell you why you might and why you might not, and what I do with weeds. I do add weeds to my *hot* compost pile but the majority have not gone to seed. I try to pull the weeds up before they have any seed heads, and it's all good as far as I'm concerned (I'm determined to have their weedy lives have some meaning).

If one or two with seeds get in there, I don't stress about it because, for the most part, hot piles fry the little seeds to death before they can rear their ugly heads again. That said, I won't throw *any* weeds into my cold pile that have gone to seed. That's just asking for trouble.

Keep in mind that some weeds propagate themselves from their rootstocks or even from pieces of root. One way to prevent this is to pull the weed and lay it on the open ground in the sun. This lets the roots dry out completely until they're all dried out— quite dead. Then you can throw them on the compost pile as a brown instead of a green.

Oh, Rats! (And Raccoons and Flies)

The problem: Rats and other wildlife are invading your pile.

The solution: If you actually find rodents or raccoons in your compost pile, there are only a few reasons why they're there. Compost might seem like a great place to hang out for pesky rodents, but the truth is the materials you're going to be tossing into your pile aren't the rat's idea of a good time. Rats prefer meat, fish, dairy products, eggs, grease, and prepared foods. These are all materials that you shouldn't be adding to your open pile anyway, so rats shouldn't be a problem.

Now, if rats have already taken up residence in your yard, they may take a peek at what you have in your compost on their nightly stroll, but you need to look for other reasons that the rats are attracted to your yard such as …

- Dog or cat food left outside
- Rabbit or chicken food left outside
- Palm trees (perfect for nesting)

♦ Uninhabited buildings in the area

♦ Unsecured garbage cans or bags

♦ Construction areas

♦ Thickly planted ivy

Raccoons will visit your yard or garden for the same reasons rats do, but they will also enjoy some kitchen scraps that *are* going to be in your pile, as well. For this reason, I put my kitchen waste into a prefabricated bin with ¼" (or smaller) holes (the tumblers are great for this, too) or my worm bin.

Invariably, you'll get some fruit flies and quite possibly houseflies. To keep them at bay, bury your kitchen waste (especially fruit) into the pile a bit. And if you're adding fresh manure, bury that as well. If you turn your pile and some manure or food scraps end up at the top, you can put a shallow layer of hay or any other brown on the top. This is another good reason to cover your open pile with a tarp. And keep in mind that the other creepy crawlers you may see in your pile are probably macroorganisms that are good for your compost pile.

Digging Deeper

Trick fruit flies into a homemade trap. Recycle a margarine tub or deli salad container and poke holes into the lid using a small Phillips screwdriver. Fill the container about a third of the way with soapy water. Add some bait such as banana peels, or other old fruit. The fruit flies will be lured to a watery death.

Playing It Safe

As with anything we do in life, there are certain risks associated with gardening and composting. Most of them can be easily avoided by taking the following simple safety measures:

♦ Wear gloves while working with compost—or doing any gardening for that matter. They ward off blisters, keep your hands from contacting any bacteria in the soil, and protect your skin from cuts.

♦ Wear shoes that cover the entire foot.

♦ Wear protective goggles when working with power tools such as hedge trimmers.

- Put on a sun hat and sun block to protect your skin from the sun's damaging and harmful rays.

- Wash your hands thoroughly with soap and warm water after handling compost or gathering organic materials—even if you were wearing gloves.

Although it's very unusual for people to become sick from handling compost, I would be remiss if I didn't mention that it is possible, particularly for people whose immune systems are compromised. Some infections and diseases that can be contracted through composting are:

- **Tetanus and lock jaw**—A toxin called *Clostridium tetani* that lives in the soil can attack the central nervous system. Be sure that your tetanus vaccination is current.

Prickly Problem

When you're turning the compost pile, loose particles or even mold spores can float through the air and can get into the lungs. If you'd like to keep any harmful materials from entering your lungs, wear a disposable facemask.

- **Farmer's lung**—Bacteria or fungal spores cause symptoms similar to pneumonia. Wear a facemask, especially if you're handling moldy hay.

- **Histoplasmosis**—The fungus *Histoplasma capsulatum*, found in many types of bird droppings, can cause respiratory infections. If you're handling bird droppings (like chicken manure) you may want to consider wearing a mask.

- **Paronychia**—This is an infection that penetrates the crevices of your fingers by your fingernail. Wear gloves to protect your fingers.

The Least You Need to Know

- Keep your pile aerated by turning it regularly, adding ventilation stacks, or laying coarse materials into the pile as you build it.

- Maintain a proper level of moisture by adding water to your pile regularly and keeping it covered.

- When the pile is too dry, add water and nitrogen (greens).

- When the pile is too wet, add air and carbon (browns).

- If wild critters are invading your compost pile, you need to find out what is attracting them.

- Use appropriate safety precautions when composting, including wearing gloves and close-toed shoes.

7

Spreading the Wealth

In This Chapter

◆ Determining when your compost is ready

◆ Making the most of your compost

◆ Raking in the benefits of leaf mold

◆ Brewing compost tea

◆ Peat moss and its environmentally friendly alternatives

◆ Taking advantage of mycorrhizal fungi

Now that you have your own compost production going, it's time to start thinking about what you're going to do with all that black gold. Which means you also need to know how to tell when your compost is ready to be used.

This chapter also introduces you to the benefits of leaf mold, compost tea, peat moss alternatives, and mycorrhizal fungi. Most of these goodies are free, and all of them are great for your garden.

When Do I Know It's Done?

You already know that compost's final stage is humus. Humus is compost that's been decomposed to the point that the microorganisms have almost completely stopped working on the organic materials in the pile. It is dark and crumbles apart in your hands. It has a fluffy texture and smells like sweet, fresh earth or the forest floor. When your compost reaches this stage, its nutrients are the most easily accessible to plant roots.

The phrase "in the eye of the beholder" applies just as well to humus as well as it does to beauty. Whether compost is "finished," and therefore ready to spread, is truly subjective. It's completely acceptable to use your compost anywhere near its final stages of decomposition.

How fast will you have finished humus? The pendulum swings very wide here. Anywhere from three weeks to one year is the reality, depending on the following factors:

- **Where you live.** Your USDA zone matters because matter tends to decompose a little faster in warmer climates (assuming your pile has moisture) and a little slower in cooler areas.

- **The type of pile you build.** Obviously, a cold pile will decompose a lot more slowly than a hot pile.

- **What you add to your pile.** Very fibrous materials like branches or corn cobs break down slowly. Veggie scraps and old straw decompose quickly. The size of the material you add also influences the decomposition time frame. The smaller the pieces, the faster the pile breaks down.

Wise Worm

Some master composters believe that compost should be aged six months or more to be sure it's broken down completely. Others do not use any time frame but instead go on looks alone. If it looks like humus, they go ahead and apply it to their soil.

If you've been intensely composting (shredding your materials, turning continuously, keeping it moist, etc.), then you can have compost in as little as three to four weeks. If you're letting nature do most of the work, it could take six months to a year—which isn't always a bad thing. The average time frame, if you're putting in a little time and basically balancing your pile with the greens and browns, is about four to six months.

The gardeners I hang around with tend to be as impatient as I am and almost never wait until their compost has hit the humus stage. As soon as we get our first whiff of sweet soil, we roll out our wheelbarrows and start spreading compost around like crazy. Even if the compost isn't fully decomposed, the plants get to reap the benefits of the compost while the microbials finish their job in the beds instead of in the compost bin.

It's also worth mentioning that sometimes compost that's used on the earlier side will have a water-repelling effect and tend to absorb water slowly. Not to worry—this phenomenon disappears quickly as the compost finishes decomposing and blends with the existing soil.

In the end, remember that while you can use compost as a basic foundation-planting medium (along with the soil that's in the garden bed), it has numerous other uses as well.

Wise Worm

Did you know compost is the best secret for successful tomatoes? Compost gives your tomato plants everything they desire. Just 2 inches of compost spread around your tomatoes will give them the winning edge on rapid production and large fruit.

Prickly Problem

One thing to be aware of is that if there's still a lot of carbon to be decomposed when you add unfinished compost to your garden, the microbes will rob some of the nitrogen from your soil to aid in the decomposition process. You can throw a little extra green material onto the bed to balance things out, but even if you do nothing, the soil will eventually balance itself out.

Screening Compost

The pictures of compost you see in gardening magazines and books portray humus as gorgeous—almost good enough to eat. The finished humus in your compost pile won't look this way—at least not without a little help by you. That's because the humus in the pictures has been screened or sifted to remove any large chunks, giving it that perfect loamy look, which also looks nice in the landscaping, by the way. It doesn't mean the compost in the pictures is any less real, but it does have its stage make-up on.

If you'd like your compost to be as pretty as a picture, you can make your own compost sifter. You'll need the following items:

1" × 4" pieces of wood

Galvanized hardware cloth

Wood screws

Power screwdriver

Saw

Staple gun

Wire cutters

Wise Worm _____

Keep several compost piles going so you can have fresh compost to use all year long.

Follow these simple steps for constructing the sifter:

1. Use a saw to cut the wood pieces into the desired length to construct either a square or rectangular frame. The size of the frame is up to you, but one option is to make the frame roughly the same size as the top of your wheelbarrow. That way you can sift the compost into the wheelbarrow and have it ready to transport to its final destination.

2. Screw the wood together with the wood screws.

3. Using wire cutters, cut the hardware cloth to fit your frame.

4. Secure the mesh to the outside edge of the frame using wood screws or a staple gun.

A homemade compost sifter.

Once your sifter is ready, place it on top of your wheelbarrow and start scooping your compost onto the screen. The finer compost will fall through the little squares into your wheelbarrow, and the larger pieces—such as twigs and chunks of undecomposed material—will stay on top of the screen. Put those bigger pieces back on the compost pile to finish breaking down.

> **Wise Worm** _____
>
> When you collect your compost to spread in the garden or landscape, don't forget to leave a little compost in the bin. Finished compost is loaded with micro- and macroorganisms. It's the perfect activator to start a whole new batch of materials for your next compost pile. In fact, you'll notice that the next pile is ready even faster than the first if you leave some of your old compost behind.

Is There Such a Thing as Too Much Compost?

You can't put too much compost on your garden or landscape beds. You're limited only by your supply. Some people recommend aiming for about 1 to 1½ pounds of compost per square foot, but that's the beginning of the scale. I add as much compost as I can to every garden bed I have.

Making Potting Soil

Compost is also the perfect base ingredient for potting soil for both indoor and outdoor plants. When you have your own compost, you can save money on prebagged potting soil by mixing up a homemade batch instead. There are many different recipes for making your own potting soil. The following recipes vary slightly in weight. Experiment to see what type you prefer and try your own hand at a potting soil mix! Use these soil mixes for outdoor as well as indoor plants.

- ⅓ topsoil, ⅓ compost, ⅓ builder's sand

- ¼ compost; ¼ builder's sand; ½ peat, coir, or rice hulls

- ¼ compost; ¼ topsoil; ¼ vermiculite; ¼ peat, coir, or rice hulls

- ⅓ compost, ⅓ garden soil, ⅓ builder's sand

- 4 parts commercial potting soil to 1 part compost

> **Prickly Problem** _____
>
> Don't forget, if you're interested in growing azaleas or other acid-loving plants, you should test the pH to be sure the soil is slightly acidic.

If you have worm castings (see Chapter 8) or leaf mold (see later in this chapter) on hand, add them to your potting soil as well. The worm castings are high in nutritional value and the leaf mold is a terrific soil stabilizer.

The Peat Moss Dilemma

Peat moss has been a favorite soil additive for many years. It's a natural product that's harvested from ancient cold-climate peat bogs in Canada, Europe, and parts of the United States. It contains beneficial bacteria as well as a natural fungicide that is a barrier to several troubling fungi including damping off, which is the bane of anyone who starts their plants from seed. In addition, peat moss is capable of absorbing 10 to 20 times its weight in water. It also allows for good drainage by lightening the soil.

Unfortunately, however, using peat (at least to excess) is no longer considered an environmentally sound practice anymore. It's considered a nonrenewable resource because, although it is *technically* renewable, it takes about 1,000 years for a peat bog to grow a single yard of peat. As a consequence, the world's peat bogs are being destroyed at a far-faster pace than they will ever renew. This causes permanent and destructive changes in their eco-systems, including the loss of habitat for creatures whose lives depend on these peat bogs.

Peat Moss Alternatives

Fortunately, there are some effective alternatives to peat that you can use in your potting mixes.

Coir

Coir (pronounced *koy-er*), also sometimes called coco-peat or coir-peat, is the hairy outside layer of husk on coconut shells. Because it's a by-product of coconuts that are grown for their meat, coir is an environmentally friendly alternative to peat. (Of course, processing and shipping coir produces pollution, so it's not the "perfect green" by that definition.)

Digging Deeper

Coir that's harvested from young coconuts is light in color (called "white fiber"). It's often used for yarn, rope, twine, mats, and sacks.

The coir used by gardeners is harvested from mature coconuts and comes in blocks that expand when soaked. Mature coir breaks down very slowly. If you want to use coir as a planting medium, be aware that there's not much nutritional value in coir by itself.

It needs to be blended with a nutritional component such as compost. You can also add a slow-release fertilizer into the mix. However, coir retains moisture extremely well and lightens the soil like peat but is much more eco-friendly than its peat counterpart. That said, peat is less expensive than coir and gardeners still purchase it.

Rice Hulls

Rice hulls are a good alternative to peat. They lighten the soil, absorb water well, and offer good drainage. Before rice grains are converted (parboiled) or polished, they are dried and then hulled. The hulls, which would otherwise be tossed out, can be used as a soil-less medium just like coir or peat. They're very thin and nearly weightless.

You can add rice hulls to potting mixes, but even on their own they have merit as a soil amendment by both aerating and retaining water. Rice hulls are a nice alternative to peat, as they are less expensive and are an easily renewable resource.

> **Digging Deeper**
>
> The old school of thought was that potting soil needed to be pasteurized. Fortunately, that's not the case. In fact, over-heating compost or soil kills the microbes that right disease, which increases the likelihood of developing pathogens in your garden soil.

No Digging Required

Because plants take up nutrition through their roots, gardeners often "dig" compost into their garden beds to place the compost directly into the root zone. While this is a perfectly acceptable practice, it's also completely unnecessary.

Night crawlers and their redworm cousins already living in the soil are perfectly capable of mixing the compost in with the soil and aerating it. These fastidious work-ers are excellent at combining your compost with the earth, so you don't have to worry about anything but getting your garden gold to the plants.

That said, some gardeners argue that it's best to mix compost into the garden soil, as the compost may dry out just sitting on top of the ground. But this should only be done *before* your garden is planted for the season.

> **Prickly Problem**
>
> If you have a weakened immune system or are preg-nant, wear gloves when handling compost. Bacterial and fungi spores working away at the materials could possibly pose a health problem for people with suppressed immune systems.

To attempt to till up the soil while your plants are actively growing could disturb their roots, hinder their growth, and possibly even kill them.

As far as timing, some people will tell you that spring, just before you plant, is the perfect time to spread compost. Others will swear by distributing it in the fall. I spread my compost any time it's ready because I consider it blasphemy to hesitate using compost that's ready to go. I compost one of my piles intensely so that I have compost ready for plants about every three to four weeks in the summer.

Top and Side Dressings

Top dressing and side dressing application techniques are ideal for landscape, flower, herb, and garden beds in which plants are already growing. When you "top dress" plants with compost, you sprinkle several handfuls of compost on top of the soil above the plant's roots. This is opposed to covering a whole garden or bed with a thick layer.

Digging Deeper

Give new or just-divided plantings a little nutritional boost by adding compost to the freshly dug hole before planting.

When you side dress compost, you dig a long, shallow trench about a foot away from the plants and place some compost inside the trench. It's a mini version of trench composting (see Chapter 6), except that instead of tossing organic materials into the trench, you add finished compost. This is the best way to be certain your plants reap the benefits without disturbing their roots.

Why We Love Leaf Mold

Some composting gardeners don't add leaves to their compost bins at all, but instead save them for a special type of compost called leaf mold. Leaf mold, like compost, smells like the forest floor—probably because it *is* the forest floor. Leaf mold doesn't offer much in the way of nutrition, but it does improve the soil's structure by adding texture. It also increases soil's ability to retain water, making it valuable as a soil conditioner.

If you have a lot of trees on your property or near your home, start a leaf compost of your own. Just gather as many dried leaves as you can and put them in a circular cage or unoccupied bin—even a black garbage bag will work. Add water to the leaves every now and again, and in a year or so you'll have perfect leaf mold to spread with your compost. If you want to speed up the process, add a nitrogen source—such as composted manure, grass clippings, or a couple handfuls of compost—to your bag of leaves. Sprinkle a little water in there, tie the bag closed, and shake it up. Cut a couple of slices in the bag for aeration and leave it alone. Six months or so later you'll have composted leaf mold.

Digging Deeper

Want to get your hands on some leaves but don't have any trees? Watch out for the piles or bags of leaves your neighbors put out by the curb in the fall and spring. The week after Halloween is the perfect time because many people fill those bags that look like giant pumpkins with leaves.

Tea Time! The Finer Points of Brewing Tea

Compost tea, made from steeping compost in water, is a turbo dose of concentrated nutrients for the soil, which in turn benefits the plants growing in the soil. It can be placed directly on the soil beneath plants or sprayed onto leaves or seedlings. Use it on a weak or sagging plant as a shot of compost pick-me-up.

Digging Deeper

The jury is still out on whether compost tea is successful as a disease suppressor. Although many gardeners and farmers stand by the claim, experts say that there's not enough scientific evidence to prove this theory. It's not clear whether the diseases are kept at bay because the plants are in overall good health due to the nutrients in the tea, or whether the tea actually fights some diseases.

Making compost tea is simple. You'll need a 5-gallon bucket or any large container that will hold water (extra points for those who recycle something), and a burlap sack, cheesecloth, or fine netting to strain the compost. Strive for a ratio of 1 part compost to 5 parts water; use more compost if you want stronger tea.

Add the compost to the burlap sack or tie it into the netting like a giant tea bag. Add the water to the container and place the bag in the water to soak for several days.

After you take your compost tea bag out of the bucket, don't forget to empty the bag into your garden. You can also jump-start a new compost pile by using the tea as an activator.

Where to Use Your Tea

You can use compost tea in a seemingly endless number of ways. Here are a few suggestions to get your creative juices flowing:

◆ Use it to water your houseplants.

◆ Give a drink to seedlings or plants that are having a hard time adjusting to a new location or that just seem sickly or weak.

◆ Pour some compost tea in a watering can, hand sprayer, or hose-attached sprayer and broadcast the tea over any large space. Spraying 5 gallons of compost tea per ½-acre of area is a great start. You may want to do this twice a year: in the spring and again in the fall.

◆ If you've started a brand-new compost bed, pour the tea into the pile to give it a boost of micro-nutritional "starter."

◆ Add compost tea to your leaf mold bag as an inoculator to get the leaves moving in the right direction.

Compost Tea and Mycorrhiza

When you use compost tea on the soil, it acts as a *biofertilizer* by inoculating the soil with beneficial fungi and bacteria. One of the most beneficial of these organisms is mycorrhizal fungi.

Mycorrhizal fungi are fungi that form a *symbiotic relationship* with the roots of plants. The fungi (as well as bacteria) feed off the material secreted by the roots of plants. The thriving fungi lures nematodes or worms, which eat some of the fungi and expel nitrogen, phosphorus, and sulphur in a plant-soluble form. Most of the nitrogen is passed on to the plant, with the nematodes keeping only a small fraction for themselves. The mycorrhiza and the plants live in perfect harmony.

Some of our gardening habits can ruin the soil's potential to provide the right environment for mycorrhiza. These include erosion, tilling, construction, topsoil removal, fertilization, and herbicide application. These and other destructive practices can completely destroy, or at the very least significantly harm, these beneficial fungi.

def•i•ni•tion

A **biofertilizer** is any type of microorganism that increase the amount of nutrients available to plants.

A **symbiotic relationship** is a situation in which plants or animals of different species live together in a mutually advantageous relationship.

The Least You Need to Know

◆ "Finished" compost is in the eye of the beholder. It doesn't have to be completed before you use it in your garden.

◆ You can use your compost as a basic planting medium, top dressing, side dressing, or to make potting soil.

◆ Leaf mold is extremely valuable as a soil conditioner.

◆ Compost tea is another product of compost that you can use as a liquid fertilizer and disease suppressor for your plants.

◆ Because peat moss is considered a nonrenewable resource, you may want to use an alternative soil-less medium.

Worm Wrangling 101: Vermicomposting

Wait! Before you cringe and close the book in disgust at the thought of keeping a passel of red worms to munch and crunch your kitchen scraps, at least read the next few paragraphs.

Worm composting, a.k.a. vermicomposting, is hands-down one of the most effective composting techniques available to gardeners. Wiggly worms are amazingly efficient compost builders, taking your kitchen scraps and creating beneficial nutrients for the soil in mere days. Furthermore, vermicomposting is easy, inexpensive, and fascinating!

So put your fears aside for a few minutes and explore the wonderful, wiggly world of worm composting.

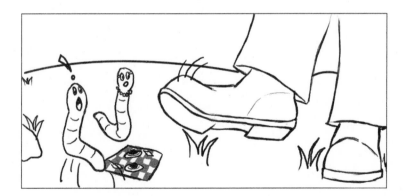

Chapter 8

Can O' Worms

In This Chapter

- Why people keep worms
- How to get past the "ick" factor
- What's so great about worm poop
- The differences among worm species
- How worms reproduce
- Worm FAQs

Vermicomposting is the practice of using worms to decompose organic waste into a nutrient-rich soil and plant product called castings. "Castings" is really just a polite way of saying "worm poop." In other words, castings are the end product of organic materials that have been passed through a worm's gut.

Worms are a huge part of the decomposition process in any compost pile. In a traditional compost pile, the worms move into the piles without any help from us. When you worm farm, however, you keep a special species of worm in a container to eat kitchen waste and turn it into a highly nutritional plant product (castings).

Why Would Anyone Volunteer to Have Worms?

It's okay to admit that up until now it hadn't crossed your mind to feed and take care of hundreds of worms. It's quite possible that for most of your life worms were right up there with gopher guts. But worms do excellent things for the earth and our plants, which makes them every gardener's best friend.

Worm castings have a nitrogen potency that's 5 times that of good topsoil, 7 times that of potash, and 1.5 times the calcium. Castings are the top of the line as far as soil amendments go.

Worm farming is perfect for people who live in apartments or condominiums who would love to have a compost pile but don't have the room. It's a portable composting system that's doable for anyone in any living situation. You keep the worms in a box-sized container or bin, which makes a large yard or garden area unnecessary. In fact, you can even keep a vermicompost system indoors.

> **Wise Worm**
>
> Cleopatra was well aware of the important role worms play in the ecosystem and had strict laws in place for anyone who hurt a worm on purpose. Rumor has it that the offender was sometimes put to death.

It's also an excellent teaching tool for school-age children learning about environmental and biological issues. Teachers the world over have used vermicomposting systems while incorporating other curricula such as science and math. (See Appendix C for more information on using vermicomposting in the classroom.)

The "Ick" Factor

Do these wiggly guys make you nervous? My advice is to go ahead and name them. Giving your worms names changes your relationship with them. They become pets, and you can't help but have at least lukewarm feelings toward creatures you've named.

> **Wise Worm**
>
> My family named our worms Freds 1 through 10,000. Although not big conversationalists (or cuddlers, for that matter) some of these little characters really stand out. Fred #422 is our spokes-worm and even has his own Facebook page (www.facebook.com/#/group.php?gid=75356045451).

As pets go, worms are not only some of the smallest around, but also the quietest creatures you'll ever care for. Plus, there's no biting, barking, scratching, shedding, or housebreaking.

All you have to do is feed them a couple of times a week. If you're truly squeamish about the amazing castings, you can provide the worm food and delegate someone else (your kids?) as the official "worm-wrangler."

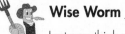 **Wise Worm** _____

> Lest you think worms don't make good pets, let me remind you that they can give as much love as the family dog can—maybe more—with their five sets of double hearts.

Worm Poop ... er, Castings

Here's the scoop on castings: while traditional composting and vermicomposting both break down organic materials and provide a terrific plant product for the garden, worms bring their own special blend to the table. Worm castings contain significantly more beneficial microorganisms, enzymes, humus, and plant stimulants than regular compost.

Worms are a gardener's best friend.

Castings offer these nutrients in high percentages in a slow-release form along with superior soil-binding, and water-retaining, abilities. They also offer excellent aeration, porosity, and structural properties. They're much higher in available nitrogen, phosphates, and potash than your average compost. Plus, these nutrients are available for a longer period of time. "Available" means that the nutrients in castings can get to the plants for easy absorption because they're water-soluble. Worm castings will also greatly improve your soil's texture.

As you know, worms are present in general garden compost as part of the breakdown in a regular heap—so you're getting castings there, too. Worm composting in a container intensifies the end product, so you have a super-charged soil amendment in bulk.

The Right Worm for the Job

When it comes to vermicomposting, not all worms are created equal. Some worms are better suited for earth-moving than for composting.

Prickly Problem

For the same reasons gardeners prefer to use Latin plant names, it's best to know the Latin name for the worms you plan to purchase. If you order a couple pounds of Giant Redworms, you might end up with a box of European night crawlers instead of the red wigglers you had hoped for. That's because European night crawlers are also commonly referred to as redworms.

Worms for Vermicomposting

The worms used in worm farming are commonly referred to as red wigglers, redworms, or manure worms. Their Latin name is *Eisenia fetida*. This is the worm species predominately used in vermicomposting systems.

Redworms are the perfect vermicomposting system tenants for several reasons. They have a voracious appetite for organic material. They're also surface-dwelling worms, which means they live most of their lives within the first 10 inches of the soil's surface. They enjoy life in areas under trees or shrubs in the leaf litter, in composts, or manures. If temperatures become unbearable for them—whether too hot or cold—they can bury themselves as deep as 2 feet underground.

Red wigglers are communal worms, meaning they live in large groups. They're capable of eating half their weight in food a day, and they reproduce quickly. Plus, they don't mind being shipped in boxes to would-be worm farmers around the world.

Wise Worm

A single redworm produces its own weight in castings in one day. In one year, an acre of worms will plow about 50 tons of soil and produce 5 tons of castings!

Although redworms are the Cadillacs of composting worms, several other types of worms perform well in vermicomposting systems as well. Among them are the Red Tiger (*Eisenia andrei*) and the Red Marsh worm (*Lumbricus rubellus*). Both of these species do a bang-up job of creating castings and are often used by commercial worm farmers.

Two other worms that are appropriate for vermicomposting are the African night crawler (*Eudrilus eugeniae*) and the Indian Blue worm (*Perionyx excavatus*); however, these worms are temperature sensitive and need a warm year-round climate.

Red wigglers and Red Tigers (*Eisenia fetida* and *Eisenia andrei*) are the most readily available for home worm bins. Your best bet is to find out which species worm farmers in your area use and go with that type of redworm.

Worms for Earth Moving

Nightcrawlers (*Lumbricus terrestris*) are often referred to as earthworms, although the term earthworm is used interchangeably with redworms as well. Nightcrawlers offer tremendous benefits to the soil in their own right, but producing large quantities of castings isn't one of them. Nightcrawlers prefer to live deep underground. They're the loners of the worm world and seem to enjoy solitude even from their own kind.

They're shy creatures and prefer to have their homes (burrows) left alone. Nightcrawlers are the muscle behind mixing the top-soils, sub-soils, and compost. Their burrowing and food hunting helps to aerate the soil and retain water by allowing water and air deep into the ground.

The Secret Love Life of Worms

Worms are masters at reproduction, and part of that reproductive success is due to the fact that they are hermaphrodites. This means that every worm carries both male and female reproductive parts—so they all have eggs as well as sperm. Even so, worms don't procreate alone—they need a mate to breed. Because individual species of worms mate differently, the following discussion of worm breeding is limited to red wigglers.

If you look closely at a worm, you might see a wide band about a third of the way down the body from the head. This is often called a saddle or a band, but the scientific word is clitellum. The presence of a clitellum indicates the worm is a mature adult capable of breeding and making baby worms.

Most worms reach mature breeding age at about 10 weeks, although it's possible for them to reach maturity at 8 weeks. These breeder worms are capable of producing 2 or 3 cocoons a week for 6 to 12 months, meaning that a single breeding worm can easily produce nearly 100 baby worms in 6 months.

When a worm reaches breeding age, they emit glandular secretions that attract a mate. Red wigglers will mate at any level of the bedding and any time of the year if they're happy with their living conditions. When two redworms find each other and fall in love (or whatever), they wiggle very close together with their heads and tails in opposite directions. The saddles (clitellum) then secrete a mucus that covers each worm. While they are covered with slimy stuff, each worm accepts sperm from the other into their receiving pouch. The sperm is held in the storage sacs until after the worms go their separate ways. Then the clitellum releases another substance that hardens and covers the outside of the band, which forms a cocoon.

At this point, the worm backs out of its saddle while depositing into the band its own eggs and the stored sperm from its mate. The eggs become fertilized, and the band seals itself off at both ends after the worm has slid out. The separate clitellum is now called an egg case, egg sac, or cocoon.

Cocoons are roughly the size of a grain of rice and are lemon-shaped. The eggs start out as white in color, changing to yellow and then light brown. When the tiny worms reach hatching age, the egg takes on a reddish cast.

Each cocoon can contain as many as 10 fertilized eggs inside it, from which one to three babies will emerge. Hatching begins after three weeks or more. When the infant worms first hatch, they're translucent white or pinkish in color and ½ to 1 inch long.

Population Control

Considering how prolific worms are, you might be wondering if your worm population will grow so large that they will eventually stage a hostile takeover of your home.

The short answer is no. There are many reasons that worms don't run the world in the wild, and they won't do so in captivity, either. Their population is utterly at the mercy of their environment.

For one thing, worms' reproductive rate is determined by the quantity of food available. As the number of castings becomes greater than the amount of food in a bin, reproduction slows to a crawl. The newborn worms begin competing for food with older worms, and as happens so often in nature, youth usually wins out. Worms also simply grow old and die of natural causes.

Also, if the conditions in their living quarters become less than ideal—such as too moist or too dry—some worms will die off. (Don't worry: dead worms decompose very quickly, so you rarely notice them.)

If you do find that your bin has had a population explosion, your best bet is to divide the current herd in half and start a second bin. Or remove a third of them to share with friends.

 **Wise Worm**

As many as 1 million earthworms can occupy an acre of soil. Earthworms can move soil particles up to 40 times their weight as they move through the earth.

Fascinating Worm Facts

Worms may live beneath our feet and seem simple in comparison to humans, but many people find worms fascinating, yet they don't really know very much about them. Here are some answers to a few common questions about worms:

Do worms have eyes?

No, worms don't have eyes, yet they do crawl away from light. They can sense light using very sensitive skin cells at the front of their bodies.

Can worms hear?

They can't actually hear sounds because they don't have ears. However, they do sense the vibrations in the soil.

Do worms chew their food?

Worms can't chew their food because they have no teeth. Worms rely on microorganisms like fungi and bacteria to help break down the food into worm bite-size particles. The redworm forages around in search of these small particles with its prostomium (a little flesh pad that hangs above the worm's mouth), feeling about until it finds something it can eat.

Once it ingests the food, it goes down to a gizzard (storage pouch) in the worm's midsection, where it's ground up by tiny bits of sand or grit the worm had previously swallowed. The muscles around the gizzard contract, mixing the grit, food, and some fluid together. Anything the worm's body doesn't digest for itself passes through its body in the form of castings.

How do they breathe?

Worms don't have lungs like people. Instead, worms respire through their body's surface. The moisture on the worm's body dissolves oxygen, which passes through the body and into the bloodstream. Without moisture, worms can't breathe and will die. While it's important to have enough moisture in the bin to keep worms' skin wet, you don't want so much in there that they drown.

Do worms have hearts?

Worms have more heart than any of us! They have five sets of double-hearts pumping their blood through their bodies. Their hearts aren't as complex as a human one, though.

How do worms move?

Worms have long muscles and circular muscles. They move by contracting and relaxing these muscles in a wave pattern. When a worm contracts the circular muscles, its body moves forward. When the long muscles are contracted, they draw the hind end of the worm toward the front end. Sometimes you'll see a worm that looks very thick. This is because when the long muscles contract, the circular muscles relax and the worm looks fat.

If you cut a worm in half, does it really grow back?

This is one myth that never dies—probably because there is some truth to it. The fact is that if you cut a worm literally in half, it won't grow its body back—it will die. However, worms are capable of regenerating a couple back end segments—but not their head. So if a little bit of a worm's rear end is cut off, it can grow back.

Digging Deeper

Worms have bristles (setae) that act like tiny brakes and hold the worm's body to the ground. You may have seen the setae in action as a bird tries to pull a worm out of the soil. Sometimes the worm will break in half because the setae are holding to the ground so tightly.

The Least You Need to Know

◆ Worm castings offer the highest nutritional value of any compost.

◆ Worms are very easy to take care of, and they don't bite, bark, scratch, or shed.

◆ Among the many different worm species, red wigglers (*Eisenia fetida*) are top performers for vermicompost bins.

◆ Worms have natural environmental population controls.

Chapter 9

Worm Husbandry

In This Chapter

- Making your own homemade worm bin
- Buying a worm condo
- Housing your worms
- Feeding your herd
- Deciding on how many worms to buy

This chapter is all about feeding your worms and giving them shelter. You'll find out what worms like to chow down on and how often, as well as what you should avoid putting in their food bowls. When it comes to worm housing, you can choose from make-in-minutes "low-income" dwellings to some pretty classy "condos." Finally, you'll get some worm shopping advice—everything from where to buy them, how many of them to buy, and how much you should expect to pay for them.

Build a Simple Worm Bin

Before you bring home your herd, you'll want to have a bin or a condo ready for them. The simplest way to create a home for your wiggly friends is to make a worm bin. This happens to be the cheapest way to start vermicomposting as well. My worms lived in a homemade bin for years before I moved them on up in the world to a worm condo.

What You'll Need

Gather the following supplies:

♦ A plastic container such as a Rubbermaid bin, readily available from any hardware store or Target

♦ A drill for making air holes

♦ Bedding, such as newspaper torn into strips, straw, leaves, or coir (coconut hull)

♦ Food, such as kitchen scraps, cornmeal, or coffee grounds

♦ Spray bottle of water

♦ Optional: 1 cup compost, dark soil, or sand (for the worm's gizzards)

How to Build Your Worm Bin

1. Drill some holes into the sides as well as the lid of the plastic container. Don't worry that the worms will see the holes and make a run for it; they're perfectly happy to stay where their food source is.

2. Add the bedding to the bin. If you're using newspaper strips, add enough to fill the bin when the paper is fluffed up. If you're using coir, you'll probably need to soak a compressed brick of the product to prepare it for the bin.

3. If you are planning to add compost, soil, or sand to the bin, do so now. If you are using a coir bedding, mix the compost/soil/sand with the coir.

4. Use your spray bottle to moisten the bed. Worms like their bedding damp—like a wrung-out sponge—at all times. If you're using coir, it should already be damp from soaking the brick. In fact, you may have to squeeze excess water out of the coir with every handful you put into the bin so it's not sopping wet.

> **Wise Worm**
>
> When worms forage for food, they have a small lip that protrudes out called the prostomium, through which worms ingest food.

5. Place the worms under the bedding then add some kitchen scraps. Sprinkle some cornmeal in there with some coffee grounds (filter, too) or tea bags. Don't overdo the food at this point because the worms won't eat as much while they're adjusting to their new surroundings.

6. Lay approximately four sheets of shredded or unshredded newspaper or a piece of cardboard on top of the entire bed. This layer needs to be wetted down like the rest. I put this last layer in place even if I have a lid for my bin. It helps keep the bin cool, moist, and dark so the worms feel free to move around.

A do-it-yourself worm bin.

Commercial Worm Homes or Condos

Commercial vermicomposting bins are not cheap, ranging in price from about $75 to $150. But there are some great reasons for purchasing a commercial model. The best thing about them is that they're made as a stackable two- or three-tray system, which makes collecting castings a cinch. (See Chapter 10 for details on harvesting worm castings.)

Another nice thing about the commercial bins is that there's a spigot at the bottom so you can easily collect the *leachate* to dilute and then distribute to your plants. There's simply no waste with these systems. These premade bins also have special screen holes premolded into the plastic, which allow for air circulation

def•i•ni•tion

Leachate is a solution formed by percolating material through a liquid solution. In this case leachate is product resulting from percolating worm castings through water.

without letting flies inside. Since I've been using the commercial condos, I've had very few fly, gnat, or fruit-fly issues.

As an added bonus, worm condos are interesting conversation pieces. More than one person has started worm farming after having spotted my commercial bin and asking me about it!

The Worm Factory 360 commercial worm condo.

(Courtesy of Cascade Manufacturing Sales, Inc.)

Worm Bedding

Basic worm bedding is organic, holds moisture well, and yet allows excess water to drain. The ideal worm bedding consists of multiple materials mixed together. Ideal worm bedding includes …

Coir (coconut fiber)	Dry leaves
Newspaper (shredded)	Straw
Wood chips	

I like coir the best. It holds moisture beautifully and it looks nice. Plus, worms don't eat it as quickly as they do newspaper, which means you don't have to replenish your bedding as often. However, the easiest bedding to use is newspaper because it's readily available to most people and in many cases, free. Many commercial compost bins come with a brick of coir; you can also find it at your local nursery or garden center. Although I prefer coir, most of the time I end up using newspaper because I always have it around.

Straw will work as bedding as well, but it dries out quickly, so you'll need to water your bedding more often. Dry leaves are a good option as well, but you'll need to mix it with another bedding material so the leaves don't mat together. It is important for oxygen to be able to circulate in the bedding.

Wood chips will work, and they provide excellent aeration, but you'll need to mix them with newspaper, coir, or leaves to maintain proper moisture levels. Your worms won't eat the wood chips as they do most of the other beddings, so go ahead and screen these out when harvesting your castings. After they've been screened, just toss them back in the bin to reuse as bedding.

Additional materials that you can add to your worm bedding include …

Compost	Rock dust
Good garden soil	Crushed eggshell
Sand	

When you blend a basic bedding material with one or more of these bedding options, you are creating the best of all worlds for your worms. Rock dust, sand, or crushed eggshells are all nice to add because worms can use a gritty substance in their gizzards to help break down other food materials.

If you're going to purchase additional material (rather than use what's available at home), rock dust is a good choice because it also discourages fruit flies from coming around by reducing the acidity in the bin.

If you can only provide basic bedding when you set up your worms' home, no worries—newspaper is excellent.

With vermicomposting, you don't have to turn the bedding like you often do with compost piles. Just feed the worms, add bedding as needed, and let them keep on keepin' on.

Digging Deeper

I keep a box of cornmeal around to sprinkle in the worm bin once in while. It's great for times when I don't have much to offer my worms in the way of kitchen waste. Also, cornmeal is the perfect first food to add to a brand-new worm bin because the particles are very small and easy for the new residents to eat.

Moisture

Worm bins need to be kept moist at all times for redworms to survive. These guys take in oxygen through their skin and need moisture to breathe. Keeping the moisture consistent involves checking the bin every couple of days and looking for dry areas that need to be moistened. Keep a spray bottle near the bin to make adding moisture as easy as a couple of squirts or add shredded newspaper that's been wetted down. Worm bins made of wood or that don't have a lid dry out more often. Also, watch for too much moisture due to heavy water content of food scraps. For more troubleshooting tips, see Chapter 10.

If you haven't checked on your worms in a while and you notice that the bin seems dangerously dry, go ahead and pour some water into the bin, letting it leach through to the bottom tray. If you have a homemade bin, pour the extra water out after a few minutes.

Wise Worm

Worms normally die within a year of being born. However, red wigglers have been known to live for up to four years.

To be sure about the moisture content in the worm bedding, take a bit of it in your fingers and give it a squeeze. If a drop of water drips out, you're in good shape.

Temperatures

Worms thrive in temperatures ranging between 60 and 80 degrees. If temperatures get much hotter or colder than that, they ingest their food much more slowly. Red wigglers can live in temperatures down to 40 degrees or even slightly lower and up to 100 degrees, but they won't be very productive and they are certainly at risk for dying.

If you live in a zone that has extreme temperatures, you have a couple of options for keeping your worms happy and healthy. During colder months, you can add Styrofoam insulation around your bins or provide supplemental heat via a birdbath heater. However, most gardeners simply bring the bin indoors, placing it in the mudroom or the kitchen. Don't worry: worm bins typically don't smell, although sometimes they sometimes attract tiny flies.

Digging Deeper

Worms are extremely light-sensitive. So if want to see them in action, place a piece of red cellophane between or over a light source in order to observe them without them wriggling away.

For temperatures reaching beyond 100 degrees, relocate the bin into a cool garage, basement, or the house until the temperatures cool down.

You never want to place your worm bin in an area that receives direct sunlight, either outdoors or indoors. Worms cannot tolerate hot temperatures or direct sun. When you're looking for a home for your worm bin, try to pick a shady spot that's close to the back door or kitchen and has good ventilation. A covered porch, garage, or basement is ideal.

Worm Cuisine

Worms love many of the same foods that we do, only they are much less picky about eating leftovers. In fact, recycled food doesn't seem bother them one bit. However, the size of the food you put into the worm bin does matter: the smaller the food pieces, the easier it is for your worms to compost it.

If you've got the time, toss some veggie scraps into a kitchen chopper before putting it in the bin. Otherwise, just chop up your scraps a little bit and put them in a container on your counter. Every couple of days, empty the container into your worm bin. It's that easy!

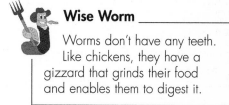

Wise Worm

Worms don't have any teeth. Like chickens, they have a gizzard that grinds their food and enables them to digest it.

Worms can get by being fed two to three times a week or less if you feed them larger quantities. You certainly won't want to keep food waste on the kitchen counter longer than a week. At first you'll need to figure out how much food and how often to feed them. This will depend on what the food is, how established your bin is, and how many worms you have. Keep in mind that in the very beginning, it's better to underfeed than overfeed the worms. You need to give your worms time to adjust to their new home and food.

What Worms Want

Nearly all kitchen waste except meat and dairy can go into the vermicompost bin.

Here's a sampling of food your worms will love:

◆ Fruit peelings and cores (apples, bananas, etc.)

◆ Cereal

◆ Vegetable peelings (potatoes, cucumbers, etc.)

◆ Grains

◆ Cake

◆ Pizza crust

- Tea bags

- Coffee grounds (filters, too)

- Bread

- Eggshells (crushed)

- Pulp from juicers

- Melon rinds

- Cornbread and meal

- Pancakes

- Lettuce

- Oatmeal

- *Tomatoes

- *Orange peels

- *Onion peels

- *Peppers

- Paper products such as napkins, and paper wrappers

*Tomatoes, orange peels, onion peels, and peppers all have asterisks by them because these items should be used sparingly in your worm bins. The worms find these materials offensive in large quantities and tend not to eat them until they are the only items left in the bin. If you overload the system with these items, they will end up rotting before the worms eat them, which will cause your bin to smell.

Wise Worm

Red wigglers love rabbit poop. So if you have some available, go ahead and use it, because rabbit poop is also an excellent source of nutrition for plants. Some people worry about the smell, but once the poop is in the bin, the worms make short work of it and the odor disappears quickly.

What Worms Don't Want

To keep your worms happy, as well as to avoid unwanted odors and pests, you'll want to avoid adding the following items to your worm farm:

- Meat and poultry
- Dairy products like milk and cheese
- Oil and grease
- Butter
- Nonfoods like plastics
- Dog and cat feces

Digging Deeper

Going on vacation? No need to hire a pet sitter for your worm farm. Just be sure to add some food just before you leave, but don't overfeed to make up for the days you'll be gone. The worms won't eat it any faster, and you could have a sloppy mess waiting for you when you come back. Just add some extra moistened bedding, then cover it with a wet piece of cardboard, burlap, or even plastic. The worms won't have any problem living off the food you gave them and munching on bedding, too. Unless you live in an area with very high temperatures and low humidity, they'll be just fine.

Worm Shopping

You can order worms from commercial worm raisers online. During your Google search, you just might be able to find a worm farm in your area. If you do locate a local supplier, try to arrange a tour of their farm. If you are excited about visiting a bona fide worm farm, your local cooperative extension office may have a list of local worm farmers. If it's a smaller operation, there probably won't be a whole lot to see, but many worm farms are quite large and very interesting. These professional worm wranglers will be able to answer all of your questions. You'll find a list of worm farms in Appendix B.

Digging Deeper

Don't forget to check your local coffeehouse like Starbucks for coffee grounds for your worms as well as for your other compost piles.

Most would-be worm wranglers purchase 1 pound of worms for their first worm bin. That's approximately 1,000 worms. It will take the worms several weeks to acclimate to their new home, but once they do, a pound of worms eats about a half pound of kitchen scraps per day. In three months, the worm population will have doubled.

Vermicomposting with Rabbits

If you happen to have rabbits either as pets, for show, or for meat, why not triple—or quadruple—your castings crop?

In addition to serving as a valuable garden fertilizer and compost pile ingredient, rabbit manure can also play a leading role in worm farming. All you do is place your worm bin directly under the rabbit cage. The red wigglers turn unused rabbit pellets and rabbit poop into dark, nutrient-rich humus. It's a popular technique practiced by many rabbit breeders.

> ### Wise Worm
> Most animal manures are "hot" manures that burn plants if directly applied to the garden without being properly aged or composted first, but not so with rabbit poop. Rabbit manure is considered a "cold" manure, in that it doesn't have to be aged at all before using it on plants as an organic fertilizer or soil amendment.

def•i•ni•tion
A **rabbitry** is where rabbits are housed together. Usually it more specifically refers to a situation where rabbits are being bred and raised.

By raising rabbits and worms together, you'll end up with ...

- High-quality vermicompost (worm castings) for your garden.
- A never-ending source of worms for fishing bait.
- Extra vermicompost and worms to sell for a profit, if you're so inclined.

In addition, you'll spend less time cleaning out rabbit cages, and with a vermicomposting system incorporated into the *rabbitry*, the worms will eliminate manure piles, minimize odors, and reduce the presence of flies.

Situating Rabbit Cages

Rabbit hutches are often built on wooden legs and have slide-out trays (pans) under the bottom of the cage wire. If this describes your rabbit hutch, remove the tray and place a worm box directly underneath the hutch to catch the manure as well as the unused pellets.

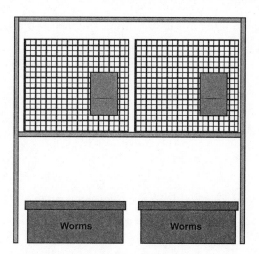

How to configure your own rabbitry worm boxes.

Some rabbit breeds may not have sufficient amounts of thick fur on the bottoms of their feet to warrant housing them on wire flooring. For example, the English Angora sometimes has very lightly furred feet and may need solid flooring to be comfortable. Very large breeds such as the French Lop are often too heavy to be comfortable on wire. Please take this into consideration when choosing housing for your rabbits.

If you have rabbit cages or hutches with a solid bottom, you can still take full advantage of the manure for worm-raising. Simply keep a portable worm box nearby along with a hand-held scoop. Shovel any rabbit poop and spilled pellets into the worm bin at regular intervals.

Start a Rabbitry Worm Box

If you already have rabbits, it's a simple matter to build a worm box under your existing rabbit cages. Plan on having 300 to 500 worms per each square foot of worm box. Weight-wise, that's about a half pound of worms per square foot. Of course, you'll also need worm bedding such as newspaper torn into strips, shredded leaves, straw, shredded documents, or seedless hay. Your worms will need this bedding to start out with until they make themselves at home in some decent rabbit poop.

You can build them from scratch or you can repurpose a wooden box for your worms. Either way, the worm box should be 4 to 5 inches wider than the cage or hutch so everything that falls out of the cage is caught by the box.

Place 3 to 4 inches of bedding at the bottom of the box. Moisten the bedding with water. When the rabbit poop is 1 to 2 inches high, mix the bedding and the manure together (carbon + nitrogen) and water it down until it's thoroughly wet, but not soaking.

You may need to sprinkle water in the worm boxes every two to three days. Every few days you should also put your hand into the box to feel if it's getting hot inside. If you do feel heat, mix everything up until it cools down. You want the bedding to be cooled down before adding your worms to the box. Now, place the worms inside the box.

Permanent boxes can be quite deep (1–3 feet). However, if you'd like to be able to move those boxes when they're full of rabbit poop, you'll want to stay closer to a foot deep.

> **Prickly Problem**
>
> If you have open worm boxes underneath your rabbit cages, you'll want to be sure to keep chickens and other worm-loving animals out of the rabbitry.

There's a couple of ways to design permanent worm boxes. The first way is to build only the sides of the worm box, leaving the bottom of the box open so that worms naturally found in your soil gravitate to the area and move in. This is of course, assuming your rabbit hutch is sitting over bare earth.

Alternately, you can build a completely enclosed bin and purchase red wigglers. It won't be long until the purchased worms create an entire colony of baby worms.

Maintaining Worm Boxes

To maintain your rabbitry worm box you need to keep it moist and avoid excessive urine.

Worms can't do anything with dry rabbit manure that's piled up on one spot. So you want to make sure the worm boxes stay moist. You'll need to give the box a spray of water every couple of days, but in the summer months, it may be more like once a day.

Keep an eye out for urine build-up in the bin. Break up heavily soiled areas with a small hand rake, mixing it into the rest of the manure. Worms tolerate the salt in urine as long as it isn't highly concentrated.

If there's quite a bit of urine, soak some of it up by tearing newspaper strips and adding some bedding. You can also scoop out the heavy urine section and toss it into your traditional compost pile—it'll be used well there.

A couple of times a month, take a pitchfork or small shovel and gently loosen all the contents in the bed so things don't get packed down.

Digging Deeper

Won't all that rabbit manure produce more flies?

In an established vermicomposting system, no. When worms are actively processing rabbit manure into compost, the flies don't have a chance to hatch before the poop becomes vermicompost.

The secret is to have as many worms as you need for the rabbit manure you're producing. If, however, you have a pile of rabbit manure in one corner that the worms can't get to, flies could be a problem. If this happens, simply knock down the manure and mix it in with the rest of the contents of the worm box.

Tips for Worm Farmers

Keeping worms isn't difficult, but there are some things you can do to simplify certain aspects of the job. The following tips are intended to help you along while you're getting used to your vermicomposting system:

- Grass clippings are fine for the bin if used in small amounts. However, if you overdo it, you'll heat up the worm bin, which is bad news for your worms.

- Dry leaves will get the worms moving at a fast clip, but add magnolia, bay, and eucalyptus leaves sparingly. Too many of these leaves can be poisonous to worms. Cedar, fir, and pine needles should be avoided, as well.

- The smaller the pieces of food, the faster your worms can ingest it.

- Watch out for foods that are spicy, salty, or acidic. They're fine for the worm bin, but use them in small amounts.

◆ When you first start your worm farm, deciding how much to feed them can be tricky. When in doubt, err on the side of less food to avoid odors and attracting flies and other pests.

◆ Want to feed your worms food that will break down in a jiffy? Put the scraps into a microwavable container with a small amount of water. Cover the container and microwave it for five minutes or so. Let the food cool before putting it in the bin.

The Least You Need to Know

◆ Commercial worm bins are wonderful, but homemade bins are easy and inexpensive to make.

◆ The ideal worm bedding consists of multiple materials as opposed to just one.

◆ Keep your worm bedding damp like a wrung-out sponge.

◆ Almost all kitchen waste other than meat and dairy can be added to your worm bin.

◆ You need about 1 pound of worms (1,000 worms) on average to start a compost bin.

◆ Raising worms under rabbit cages gives you worm castings for your garden, worms you can use for fishing, and saves time by doing less rabbit-cage maintenance.

Chapter 10

Harvesting Worm Castings

In This Chapter

- ◆ Harvesting worm castings
- ◆ Making use of vermicompost
- ◆ Brewing worm tea
- ◆ Troubleshooting worms

In this chapter, you'll learn how to separate your worms from their castings in order to harvest vermicompost. And once you have your "worm gold" stash in hand, you'll find out about the many ways to put it to work for your plants—outdoors as well as indoors. In addition, you'll learn some great troubleshooting tips for handling the most common problems associated with raising worms, as well as a great recipe for fattening up some of your herd for the fishing pole.

Getting Worms to Give Up the Goods

When you start to see a lot of dark, rich material that resembles good soil in your worm bin, you can begin harvesting castings. At this point you have two options: you can either stop feeding the worms for a week or two and let them finish the last of the food (and bedding), or you can take what's not yet decomposed and put it aside to add back to the bin.

Either way is perfectly acceptable. However, if you decide to wait for the worms to completely convert the bin's contents to castings, you'll end up losing worms to starvation—maybe most of them—for a while, anyway. When you restart the bin, the worms will begin reproducing quickly, replenishing their population.

You have several techniques at your disposal for collecting your garden gold. All of them involve separating your worms from their castings. Let's begin with the fastest method.

The Fast Way

For the fast way of sorting worms from castings you'll need the following supplies:

◆ A tarp or thick sheet of plastic (just large enough to hold lots of small piles of castings)

◆ A bright light, preferably with a 100-watt bulb

◆ A container to temporarily hold separated worms

◆ A container to hold the harvested worm castings

◆ A plastic hand scoop

Sorting worms from castings using a tarp and a light.

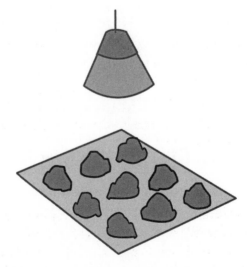

Spread the tarp out on the ground. Using the scoop, remove a small pile of worms/castings from the worm bin (a true worm wrangler will probably just use his or her hands) and make piles of the worms/castings all over the tarp—it'll look like a bunch of little mounds of coffee grounds. Place the light directly over the piles on the tarp. If you're using a lamp, you may want to remove the shade—possibly even suspending it over the worms.

Because worms will immediately begin to move away from the light, they'll burrow down into the little vermicompost piles. After about 10 minutes, there won't be a worm in sight. Scoop off enough of the castings in each pile so that you see more worms. Once again, wait a few minutes while the worms move even closer to the very bottom of the pile and onto the tarp.

Digging Deeper _____

If children are helping with the harvesting, they don't usually wait for the worms to entirely disappear, but end up hand-separating the worms from the compost. This works, too, so let the kids get involved.

Wise Worm _____

Just for fun, weigh the worms you pull out of the bin. To calculate the growth of your herd, subtract however many pounds you started with from the current weight. I think you'll be impressed with the growth of your worm herd.

After you've gathered most of the castings, pick up the worms and put them in a separate container.

Repeat the process until you've removed all the contents from the worm bin.

After the harvest is complete, add fresh bedding to your worm bin and place your herd back inside their home to begin the vermicomposting process all over again.

If you have more worms than you'd like or need, take about half of your worms and start a second bin. Or make a gift, along with a bin and bedding, for a family member or close friend. Keep in mind that many elementary schools would appreciate one as a science project for the classroom.

The Lazy Way

The simplest way to harvest castings is to let the worms separate themselves without you having to lift a finger. When the bedding is pretty well devoured and it's at the point where you'd need to add more, push all of the finished castings to one side of the worm bin. Next, add a small amount of bedding to the side without the castings.

Take some food and bury it in the new bedding, but don't add anything at all to the vermicompost side. Finally, cover only the side with the new bedding and food with sheets of newspaper or cardboard. Your goal is to make the "new" side a more pleasant worm hangout. After about two weeks, most of the worms will have migrated to the newer side of the bin, leaving the finished castings behind for you to harvest.

You will end up harvesting some worms along with the castings, but because you're adding the material to your garden, that's perfectly okay.

The Condo Way

If you have a commercial bin with three stacking trays, harvesting castings is a snap. It works like this:

Place the first tray with the worms, bedding, and food onto the bin stand. As the worms eat the food and the bedding, the tray becomes full of castings. As the castings fill up that tray, add the second tray, filled with more food and bedding, above the first tray. The worms will migrate up through the holes in the grid to the second tray in search of food. Once most of the worms have migrated, pull out the bottom tray to harvest the castings. It's a cool process, and once you've used it, you may find yourself smitten.

Prickly Problem

When using the tray-stacking system be sure that the material in the bottom tray is in physical contact with the next tray before you stack it on. Worms can't jump and the material volume is reduced as it's eaten, causing a gap in between trays that prevents the worms from moving up to the next level.

How to Use Castings for Plants

Now that you've harvested this wonderful stuff, what do you do with it? The first thing you'll notice is that you have much less vermicompost to work with compared to the amount of compost you reap from an outdoor compost bin. This means you might want to be a little more selective about what you do with it. Rather than just spreading the stuff randomly in your garden and flower beds, as you might do with compost, you probably want to reserve your vermicompost for plants that need the nutrition the most. The good news is that a little vermicompost goes a long way. You don't need truckloads for plants to reap its benefits.

Prickly Problem _____

Although the nutrition in vermicompost is available to your plants immediately, you can also store the vermicompost for later use. The key is to keep it moist, as it's hard to rehydrate the stuff once it has dried out. One way to keep it damp is to store it in Ziploc baggies.

Castings for Planting, and as a Top Dressing

Although it's perfectly acceptable to add soil amendments to your garden and beds at any time of the year, it only makes sense to add anything high in nutritional value while plants are actively growing. When you pump up plants with vitamins, they tend to want to grow.

Most people apply castings to the soil in the spring and summer. This is also the time when the plants can make the most use out of the excellent water-holding properties of the vermicompost.

Vermicompost is perfect for the vegetable seedlings you started in early spring that need to go into their permanent bed in the garden. Just take a handful and drop it into the hole you dig for the seedling and cover it up.

If you'd like to use it on plants that are already in the ground, apply it as a top dressing at the _drip line_ of the plants. This is where the plant's tiny roots take up water and nutrition to the plant. When the water drips onto the castings, the nutrients from the castings are released into the soil, where the plants can then make use of it.

Prickly Problem _____

Adding nutrients to plants in the dead of winter in cold climates is just plain cruelty, as the nutritional boost might induce a growing spurt, but the new shoots will quickly succumb to the cold and frost.

def•i•ni•tion _____

The **drip line** is the circumference of the plant that starts at the longest outward branches.

Castings for Seed Starting

Vermicompost is terrific for starting seeds because its rich nutrients help support the new seedling's growth. While you're planting seeds in your garden, just sprinkle it along the trench you made for the seeds. If you're starting seeds indoors in trays or pots, add a little bit to the seed-starting soil.

Castings for Houseplants

Houseplants are an ideal recipient of castings because you can amend the plants year round. Simply take a small amount of potting soil out of the plant's pot and sprinkle ¼–½ inch of castings onto the soil. Your plants will absolutely love you if you do this every other month or so.

Don't Forget the Leachate

Leachate is a solution created by water running through a medium. You'll find leachate at the very bottom of your worm bin. If you're keeping your worm herd in a commercial worm condo (tray-stacking system), it'll be in the bottom tray. Often the commercial bins have a spigot attached to the lowest tray for easy worm tea collection.

The leachate contains highly concentrated organic matter, especially nitrogen and phosphates, as well as the antifungal and nutritional properties of worm castings. To use the leachate you'll need a bucket and water. Pour the leachate into the bucket and dilute it with water by at least 50 percent.

You'll want to get some oxygen into the mixture by either splashing it around inside the bucket or pouring it from one container to another. The oxygen boost causes a bloom of good bacteria. Whatever you do, don't use pure leachate on plants. This is the equivalent of spilling concentrated commercial fertilizer on your lawn, and doing so will fry your plants. After it's been diluted, gardeners like to spray the leachate directly onto their plant's leaves or pour it into the soil.

Worm Tea

You can brew your own worm tea from a handful of the castings. For brewing worm tea from castings, you'll need …

- 5-gallon bucket or some other large container (the size depends on how much tea you want to brew)

- 1 or more cups of worm castings

- Cheesecloth, burlap, or netting

- Rubber band or twine

- Water

Begin by taking 1 cup (or more) of castings and wrapping them in the cheesecloth, burlap, or netting, and securing the end with either a rubber band or twine. Fill the bucket with a gallon of water per 1 cup of castings. Steep the bag of castings in the bucket of water overnight. The next day, aerate the solution by mixing or shaking it up before applying it to the garden bed or potted plants. Some gardeners use a small aquarium pump and hose to aerate the worm tea mixture.

Compost tea has a relatively short—12- to 15-hour—shelf life. If you've shared some with the plants already and need to find a place for the rest of the brew, dump it onto your compost pile. Vermicompost tea makes an excellent compost activator for your traditional outdoor compost.

Vermicompost Troubleshooting

While vermicomposting is an extremely simple way to compost, you may run into a little snag here and there. It's a good idea to check on your bin every couple of days to make sure everything is going smoothly—especially because, unlike an outdoor pile, you'd like to keep your worm friends alive. Also if your vermicomposting system is indoors, you'll want to head off any imbalance so you don't have unpleasant odors or pests.

Is Worm Poop Supposed to Smell Like That?

The problem: Your worm bin has a strong odor coming from it.

The solution: Odors can be due to a lack of air circulation or adding too much—or the wrong kind of—food. First, try adding fresh bedding to the bin and turning the vermicompost to get the air flowing through it.

In addition, back off a little on how much food you're adding, and double-check the types of foods you've been feeding your worms. Even a little butter or grease can get smelly (animal products are a no-no), as can foods such as orange peels, which take a long time to break down. If you find such items in your bin, try to remove as much of them as you can and cover the rest of it with new bedding.

Bins may also become smelly when they are too wet. Just add some dry bedding and mix it up with the wet stuff to get things to dry out.

It's Awfully Dry in There

The problem: The bedding dries out very quickly.

The solution: Your bin isn't retaining moisture well. Spritz it all down with water and then cover it with cardboard, burlap, 100 percent cotton, or even a piece of plastic before you put the lid back on.

If you find that your worm bin is dry a lot of the time, consider changing the bedding you're using. For instance, pure straw is very hard to keep damp, so add another type of bedding, such as newspaper or coir, to the straw.

My Worms Are Dying!

The problem: You notice quite a few dead worms all at once.

The solution: Your bedding might be too dry … or too wet. If the bedding is too dry, the worms can't breathe and they'll suffocate. If it's soaking wet in the bin, they could be drowning. Also, when most of the bedding and food has turned to castings and there's nothing left to eat, your worms will die of starvation. Add some more bedding and food.

Where Did Those White Worms Come From?

The problem: You notice tiny white worms in your bin (they don't have that pinkish tinge like the redworms).

The solution: They're most likely pot worms. It's normal for some of these guys to be hanging around the bin, taking a small bit of food where they can get it. They won't harm your red wigglers. If there's a population explosion of pot worms, it's probably because there's some food in the bin that the redworms aren't consuming. Simply remove that food source and as many of the pot worms as you can along with it and things will come into balance again. There will probably be a few white worms left in the bin, but that's okay.

My Bin Is Swarmed with Fruit Flies and/or Gnats

The problem: Your worm bin is attracting a lot of fruit flies and/or gnats.

The solution: Even though fruit flies aren't going to harm anything, they are a nuisance, and most people don't want them hanging around. When you add food—

especially fruit—bury it deep into the bedding. Covering the top of the bedding with dry leaves seems to help deter fruit flies as well, as does a thick layer of anything else over the top of the bedding.

Most flies of any sort ignore clean newspaper or cardboard as far as places to lay eggs. Some composters add rock dust, which is slightly acidic and wards off fruit flies. Also be sure that your storage container on the counter, where you keep your kitchen waste until you dump it in the worm bin, has a lid. Otherwise, you could inadvertently bring the gnats or other pests to your worm bin this way. You may see other fly-type creatures as well, and the same rules apply.

My Bin Has Ants, Mites, and Other Creepy-Crawlies!

The problem: My worm bin has ants.

The solution: Put sticky ant traps by the bin's legs. You can also try putting each leg of the bin in its own water dish—ants can't swim.

The problem: My bin has mites.

The solution: Several different types of mites can be found in a worm bin at any time. They may be brown, reddish, or white. None of them will wipe out a worm farm, and some of them cause no harm at all. Regardless, it would be a fairly daunting task to remove every mite from the bin. The best thing to do is to keep your bin balanced with a steady amount of food, and wet like a wrung-out sponge, and your worms will do just fine.

Soldier fly larvae often make their way into worm bins as well. They're about the size of a quarter and rather flat, and while they look prehistorically creepy, they don't cause any real harm. They do eat some of the food that was meant for the worms. However, they become soldier flies as adults and are welcome pollinators in the garden.

Soldier flies are good pollinators for the garden.

(Courtesy of Julie Haas-Wajdowicz.)

Setting Worms Free

People sometimes wonder if they can set the red wigglers free in their garden should they ever decide they no longer want to maintain a worm bin.

It really depends. Worms will do just fine if you deposit them in an area that stays relatively damp and has lots of organic materials for them to munch on. An area that has moisture along with a lot of leaf litter is a great place for redworms, as is a loamy vegetable bed that's been amended.

An outdoor compost pile that you're keeping somewhat damp is an ideal place for red wigglers to set up home. They'll love it there and continue to break down materials in that pile, as well. But the fact is, *Eisenia fetida* truly isn't a soil dweller, and if the organic material disappears, they'll die. Which means, if they're set free on top of a dry, hardpan soil, they'll certainly die. Your goal should be to improve all of your garden soil through composting so that the worms who do thrive in soils become prolific.

Worms for Fishing

Any fishing aficionados in your family may want to use your worm farm in another way: to raise fishing worms. Most people think of night crawlers as fishing worms, but redworms are just as useful for the angler and maybe even more so. Usually, when an earthworm is put on a hook and tossed into the water, it dies very quickly. Redworms, however, are capable of staying alive for several days and continue to wiggle on the hook.

You can generally fatten up your worms by giving them cornmeal every day. You can also focus on a group of worms that are earmarked for next week's fishing expedition and power feed them with a worm fattener recipe. The following recipe is from The Worm Factory:

- ◆ 5 parts chicken layer mash
- ◆ 2 parts wheat or rice bran
- ◆ 1 part agricultural lime
- ◆ 1 part wheat flour
- ◆ 1 part powdered milk

Mix all the ingredients together and add them to your worm box. The worms will be ready for the end of your fishing pole in about a week.

The Least You Need to Know

♦ You can be as active or passive as you want to be when it comes to harvesting worm castings.

♦ Castings are great for planting, as a top dressing, seed starting, and houseplants.

♦ Worm tea is excellent for plants and as a compost activator for your outdoor bin.

♦ Most of the other critters you may encounter in your worm bin aren't going to hurt anything.

Part 3

Creative Composting: Beyond the Bin

At its most basic, composting is really just a way of recycling any type of organic material into a usable form for plants. Because grass clippings are organic material, it makes perfect sense to "grasscycle" them for reuse in your lawn or garden. It's a simple process that saves you time and money while also improving the health of your yard.

You'll also learn about the many benefits of recycling grass and leaves as mulch in your garden and landscape beds. Composting, loosely defined, is recycling organic materials into a usable form for plants and other life. All of the following techniques do exactly that and more.

The more composting techniques you incorporate into your yard and garden, the better off you, your plants, and the earth will be!

11

Composting in Bed: Sandwich or Sheet Composting

In This Chapter

- ◆ Building a compost sandwich
- ◆ Simple sheet composting
- ◆ Giving your new vegetable or flower beds a head start
- ◆ When to start planting

In this chapter, you'll discover some other excellent ways to compost without a bin or container. In fact, you don't have to do a thing to this compost once you've put everything in place.

What's a Compost Sandwich?

A compost sandwich doesn't taste nearly as good as it sounds. A compost sandwich consists of multiple layers of organic materials (greens and browns) directly on top of the garden bed.

This composting technique is perfect for someone looking to start a new garden bed on rock-hard ground. If you're planning on sacrificing a section of lawn to start a garden, this soil-amending style is exceptional. Between the microbes, macrobes, and earthworms, your once nutritionally poor land will be transformed into a fertile and loamy garden bed.

A garden that's started with a compost sandwich will have excellent water-retaining capabilities, thus making terrific use of any rainfall. The bed will have few, if any, weed problems. If a few weeds do appear, they'll slide easily out of the crumbly soil.

Everything but the Kitchen Sink!

Compost sandwiches are made from the same ingredients found in a traditional compost pile. You'll need all the browns and greens you can get your hands on.

Many sandwiches are larger than traditional compost piles, so you need to get creative when gathering ingredients.

Here's another time when Halloween season comes in handy: many people decorate for the fall holiday with hay bales. They'll need to find a way to dispose of those bales after the spooky festivities are over.

Ask a local horse stable if they have any grass hay (without seed in it) that the horses can't eat due to mold. Better yet, if you can score straw that's been used as horse bedding, you've really hit the jackpot! You'll have gathered browns and greens in one fell swoop.

A compost sandwich.

How to Make a Compost Sandwich

Here's what you're going to need to make your compost sandwich:

- **Cardboard**—flattened corrugated boxes or any other kind you have on hand

- **Newspaper**—the more, the better

- **Carbon (brown) materials**—the wider the assortment, the better. Browns include straw, leaves, newspaper, shredded bark, wood shavings, weedless grass hay, and 100 percent cotton fabric.

- **Nitrogen (green) materials**—again, you'll want a variety of these for the best results. Try grass clippings, vegetable peelings, perennial plant prunings, coffee grounds, tea bags, and seedless weeds.

- **Manure** from herbivores (or near herbivores) such as chickens, rabbits, horses, and so on (not from dogs or cats).

- **Water**

- ***Topsoil**

- ***Compost from another pile**

*These last two items are desirable but quite optional.

1. Start by cutting down all foliage, as close to the ground as you can get, and just leave it lying there. Don't rake it up or haul it way—just knock it down.

2. Cover the entire future garden bed with cardboard. Make the first cardboard layer about 2 inches thick, but don't worry about being exact. Wet down this layer.

3. Add a layer of newspaper about 10 sheets thick. Wet all of this down.

4. Next, add a layer of green materials. Use whatever nitrogen sources you have on hand, but if you use grass clippings, keep this layer on the thin side—between 1 and 2 inches. For most of the layers, you'll be aiming for 3 to 4 inches thick. Add enough water to moisten this layer.

Wise Worm

Watering in between the layers of the sandwich is important because it jump starts the decomposition process and holds the small pieces together—think of it as the mayonnaise on your sandwich. Just like any compost pile, you'll want to keep your compost sandwich damp.

5. Add a layer of animal manure if you have some available. Add water.

6. If you are adding topsoil or compost, do so at this point. Add more water.

7. You've now come full circle to the next carbon layer. You can use the newspapers again or use a different type of brown, such as straw. Repeat steps 2 through 6 until you achieve your desired height. Just make sure that the last layer is either topsoil or any type of brown.

Make the pile as tall as you'd like, although ideally it should at least be a couple of feet high. Most compost sandwiches range from 2 to 4 inches high.

Some gardeners like to "activate" their compost by adding blood meal or another source rich in nitrogen. The best activator you can add is compost from another pile.

Prickly Problem

Grass clippings layered more than 2 inches thick tend to form a matted clump, which keeps the air from circulating through it.

Wise Worm

Keep in mind that there's no need to measure or weigh any of the materials in your compost sandwich. Precision is so overrated with most gardening techniques. Make your best guestimates and let nature do the rest!

If you have another compost bin or pile going, just take some content from there and sprinkle or layer it throughout the sandwich. If you're just adding one layer of compost, make the compost the top layer. Stand back and admire your handiwork; it should look like a big, soggy sandwich. You've done good. Now leave it alone. Unless it needs some water, don't do a thing to it all winter. You're going to be thrilled with the soil in your new bed next year!

Your growing zone and the weather will play a large part in determining when, the following year, your sandwich will be ready to plant in. Generally, however, if you make a compost sandwich at the beginning of October in areas with milder winters, such as zones 8 through 10, you'll have compost in about six months. In areas with colder winters, such as zones 2 through 4, it'll be closer to nine months.

Compost Under a Sheet

Sheet composting is a variation of sandwich composting. You place the compost ingredients under a sheet of weed barrier or heavy-gauge black plastic.

To compost under a sheet, gather organic materials like grass clippings, dry leaves, straw, weeds, compost, manure, newspaper, and so on. Switching between browns and greens, layer all of the materials onto the bed you're amending. Aim for a sandwich about 6 inches thick, if possible.

Cover the compost sandwich with the sheet, securing the corners (and edges, if necessary) with bricks, stakes, or whatever works for you. To be certain that water can reach the materials underneath, poke some random holes in the plastic. Now, leave it alone for at least several months.

Wise Worm

When you make a compost sandwich, the decomposers tend to rob the nitrogen that's already in the soil beneath the organic materials in order to break down the carbons. To help balance out the equation, add extra greens, blood meal, or good manure.

Digging and Tilling Is So Yesterday

With sandwich or sheet composting, you don't need to dig or till it into the pre-existing soil either during the decomposition process or after it's all ready to be planted. If you absolutely feel the urge to do so, by all means—knock yourself out. But it's a completely unnecessary step. The earth-moving job belongs to the worms who have moved into your bed, and they take their work seriously.

Digging Deeper

Another way to sheet compost is to use only one layer of material. Gather as many dried leaves as possible and spread them 3–4 inches thick over your garden bed. With this method you'll do just a little digging. With a spade shovel, dig the leaves in just enough that they are pressed into the soil so they stay put for the winter. Leave the bed alone until spring. The leaves will give your soil a lovely, crumbly texture.

Instant Compost Sandwiches

If you're in the middle of planting season as you're reading this and you just can't wait to build a compost sandwich, not to worry. All you need to do is build your sandwich as described above, but this time add in something extra.

For a spring sandwich, you'll want to be sure to alternate your materials with layers of topsoil. Some gardeners add a layer or two of peat moss or its more earth-friendly alternatives such as coir or rice hulls. After the sandwich is built, layer the entire area with about 4 inches of topsoil. Then go ahead and plant to your heart's desire. Planting into a compost sandwich has recently been dubbed "lasagna gardening."

You'll have a wonderful soil amendment in the making for future crops, but didn't have to sacrifice the space while waiting.

The first year of crops planted in the lasagna bed will be good, but the second year's crop will be fantastic. By this time, much of the original soil will be amended and rich with worms, making an ideal environment for plants' roots to spread and thrive. Also, keep in mind that when you put your garden to bed for the season, you can sheet compost over it again.

Prickly Problem

Most compost sandwiches are built outside of any type of bin; it's basically an open compost pile. This is something to think about when deciding where to put your kitchen waste, as wildlife will be able to rummage through your sandwich. I suggest putting all kitchen scraps into an enclosed compost bin.

The Least You Need to Know

◆ A compost sandwich has the same ingredients as any compost pile.

◆ You don't have to turn compost sandwiches or sheet compost.

◆ There's no digging or tilling involved with a compost sandwich.

◆ You can plant directly into a compost sandwich as soon as you make it just by adding extra topsoil.

Chapter 12

Grasscycling

In This Chapter

♦ The many benefits of grasscycling

♦ Grasscycling myths

♦ Why your neighbors just might copy you

♦ A few words about lawn mowers

You already know the value of adding grass clippings—those nitrogen-rich "greens"—to your compost pile. Grasscycling is a terrific alternative to gathering grass clippings for your compost. It involves leaving the trimmings on your lawn to decompose right there on the spot. Grasscycling is an often-overlooked and seriously underused nutritional resource for yards.

By leaving your clippings on your lawn after you mow, you'll be doing your yard, your pocketbook, and the environment a huge favor.

The Benefits of Not Gathering Grass

All too often homeowners and lawn service companies gather their grass clippings. They either collect the clippings in a bag attached to the mower or they rake up the clippings after they mow. They then bag the clippings and haul them away, often to a landfill.

What a waste of an excellent nitrogen resource for your lawn or compost pile!

Grass clippings have a lot to offer the soil and, in particular, your lawn. After the clippings fall onto the grass, they dehydrate and decompose quickly. The clippings return to the soil nutrients (predominately nitrogen, phosphorus, and potassium).

Prickly Problem

Grass clippings comprise more than 20 percent of the waste in landfills! So by leaving your clippings on the ground you're helping ease the strain on landfills. You're also naturally recycling and making the earth (soil) more nutritious for plant life.

Wise Worm

According to one study, gardeners who switched to grasscycling when they mowed saved 30 to 35 minutes on their mowing time.

Your wallet benefits, too. Not only do you save bucks by not having to pay to have the clippings hauled away, but you'll save money on fertilizer, as well. How? Grasscycling reduces the need to chemically fertilize your lawn by as much as 25 percent! In addition, lawns that are replenished with their own clippings tend to have fewer weeds and pests, which means fewer (if any) applications of pesticides and herbicides.

The most obvious benefit of grasscycling is also the most aesthetically pleasing: your lawn will look marvelous. It will be richer, fuller, and greener.

And in a society in which people are always trying to squeeze an extra 30 minutes out of the day, grasscycling is a perfect time-saving technique. By not having to dump mower bags or rake the lawn after you mow, you shave huge chunks of time off your weekly lawn-care chores.

Grasscycling Tips

This just may be the easiest "cycling" you ever do in your life. All you need to do is make sure your grass is dry when you mow it, and make sure your mower blades are adjusted to ⅓ inch, so you're only cutting the top third of your lawn. Make sure there's no bag attached to the mower, and start mowing. It's that simple.

By keeping the blades set to ⅓ inch and only mowing your lawn when the grass is dry, you'll avoid clumps of grass clippings. The short clippings left on the lawn will be unnoticeable.

The shorter blade setting may leave your grass a little longer than you're used to. But a little longer is better. When grass is cut short, the roots focus on growing the cut blades out again, which stresses them and leaves them susceptible to disease and pests.

Longer grass blades also shade the soil and grass roots so more moisture is retained, meaning that less water is required. Also, longer grass blades crowd out weeds and block out the light that weed seeds need in order to grow.

Other tips for a healthy, grasscycled lawn are as follows:

◆ **Don't overwater your lawn.** Overwatering (especially light and frequent watering) leads to shallow roots and encourages disease and lawn pests. Watering your lawn deeply and less frequently is superior than the average few minutes every day. Of course, the amount of water necessary also depends on your soil type, climate, and the type of grass you have in your yard.

◆ **Don't overfertilize your lawn.** Overfertilizing causes excessive top growth of the lawn for no good reason other than to keep you in shape with more mowing. Keep in mind that grasscycling is going to do a lot of the fertilizing for you; if you really feel the need to continue fertilizing, use small amounts infrequently.

◆ **Keep lawn mower blades sharp.** Sharp blades are the key to a nice-looking lawn. Ragged and shabby blades leave behind a ragged and shabby-looking lawn. In addition, the uneven cut can quickly open your lawn up to disease and pests. If you're mowing with a reel mower (without a motor), razor-sharp blades will make the lawn easier to cut.

> **Wise Worm**
>
> Grass growing in a shady area needs more surface area in order to grow (photosynthesize) and stay healthy. In shady areas, compensate for the lack of light by leaving the blades a little longer when you mow. Lawns in the sun receive plenty of light and can therefore be cut shorter.

The Thatch Myth

Somewhere along the line somebody decided that when grass clippings are tossed on top of lawns, they cause thatch issues. Thatch is when organic matter accumulates below the grass blades on the soil surface.

You'll be happy to know that this myth is false. The primary cause of thatch problems in lawns is roots, rhizomes, and stems of grass. These plant parts contain large amounts of fibrous material called *lignin*, which have a difficult time breaking down and do so very slowly. In small amounts (up to about a half

> **Digging Deeper**
>
> During the summer months when it seems like the grass clippings never end, leave half of the clippings on the lawn and add the other half to your compost pile.

inch), thatch can help prevent evaporation in lawns. But any more than that and it can interfere with the lawn's drainage and begin to smother it.

Grass clippings are made up of about 80 percent water and do not cause thatch problems. Certain grass varieties, such as Bermuda and Kikuyu, are especially prone to thatch.

Won't It Spread Disease?

Grasscycling doesn't promote or spread disease any more than traditional lawn-mowing practices. If a lawn has a disease infestation, it'll be there whether you grasscycle or remove the clippings. In fact, most disease is encouraged by overwatering and improper fertilizing practices.

What Will the Neighbors Think?

Gardeners new to grasscycling are suspect of the practice of not picking up the garden waste left behind by their mowers. Their concerns vary. They wonder if their lawns will be the scourge of the neighborhood, sending the lawn police racing to their door any minute. Some are afraid to risk being shunned by tongue-wagging neighbors.

Let me put your fears to rest. What people are actually going to be wondering is how the heck you get your yard work done so quickly and what you're doing to your lawn to make it look so green and healthy. If you use a motorless reel mower, they're also going to notice how quiet and peaceful their weekend mornings are—and so will you!

Still aren't sure this will work? Call your city or county and ask about any local parks, golf courses, and sports fields that are already being grasscycled. Then go take a look at them and see what you think. You'd be surprised at how many communities have already adopted grasscycling.

Pick a Mower—Any Mower

You can grasscycle with any type of lawn mower. There's no reason to go out and purchase a new mower for grasscycling. Gas-powered lawn mowers work perfectly fine, as do electric or old-fashioned reel mowers. That said, some mowers turn grasscycling into an art.

Nonmotorized Reel Mowers

These mowers should look familiar to you—but don't be fooled: they aren't your grandfather's mower. Reel mowers have some very pleasant benefits. They generate no fumes because they don't use gasoline. There's very little noise—just a soft, relaxing clipping sound—because there's no motor. Perhaps the most superior argument in favor of reel mowers, at least as far as the lawn is concerned, is that they cut grass blades with a scissorlike motion as opposed to rotary mowers that shred the grass while mowing. Because this grass-cutting technique cuts grass blades with clean and precise motion, the plant disturbance is minimal. Traditional lawn mowers literally bruise the grass blades with their tearing motion and make the top of the grass blades to turn brown.

No emissions whatsoever, no noise pollution, naturally composting—it doesn't get much more environmentally friendly than that!

The downside for some is that they require a little more effort to use than gas-powered mowers or electric mowers, although the modern versions aren't nearly as difficult as their antique ancestors. The hardest part is getting them going, but once you're in motion they are easy to push.

Reel mowers are recommended for gardeners with lawns 6,500 square feet or less. They are not recommended for lawns made of Bermuda grass or St. Augustine grass, both of which tend to have a lot of thatch buildup. Because reel mowers are human-propelled, you can expect mowing to take a few more minutes than you're used to. On the other hand, if you're grasscycling, you aren't raking or emptying baskets of clippings, which saves you time. Reel mowers have a huge price range. You'll find them priced anywhere from $90 to $500.

Fiskars Momentum Reel Mower.

(Courtesy of Fiskars.com)

Mulching Mowers

Mulching mowers are power (gas or electric) mowers with special blades that recut clippings about a dozen times before they ever hit the ground. Mulching mowers are the very best system you can get as far as grasscycling goes. The tiny pieces of grass are forced into the soil, becoming virtually invisible. Mulching mowers are priced between $200 and $500.

Electric Mowers

Electric lawn mowers cut lawns the same way as their gas-powered cousins but without gas emissions. They're easy to start and quieter than gas mowers. Some models have long cords, but there are several cordless models (battery powered) on the market as well. An extra perk is that some municipalities and public agencies offer rebates for electric mulching mowers. Electric mowers run between $200 and $500.

What If You Hire a Lawn Service?

If you hire a lawn service to care for your lawn, ask them to start grasscycling when they mow your lawn. Many lawn services would embrace the practice if they know their customers support it. If they've never done it before, ask them to treat your lawn as their "beta" version.

The Least You Need to Know

- By grasscycling, you'll naturally be fertilizing your lawn.
- Grasscycling saves you time, money, and energy—and it's good for the environment.
- Grasscycling doesn't cause thatch, disease, or make your yard look ugly.
- Special mowers are designed to help you grasscycle.

Magnificent Mulches

In This Chapter

- ◆ The mulch-compost connection
- ◆ The many benefits of mulching bare soil
- ◆ How and when to use mulch
- ◆ Which mulches are best for what garden areas
- ◆ Living mulches

In this chapter, you will learn about the many merits of mulching. Just like the other composting methods you've learned about so far, applying organic mulch to garden and landscaping areas adds humus to the soil—and that's *always* a good thing.

The Many Uses of Organic Mulch

Organic mulches are formerly living materials laid down on top of the soil in a garden or landscape area. When the material eventually breaks down, it becomes compost, offering organic matter to the soil and the plants. The only difference between mulching and traditional composting is how the material is used until it decomposes.

Wise Worm

Mulching saves, time, money, water, and your back. Mulch is valuable in any type of gardening situation. Use it in your landscaping, vegetable beds, herb garden, flower garden, perennial beds, and under trees. When you get into the habit of mulching all of the planted areas in your yard, it's entirely possible that you'll never have to spend a dime on herbicides again.

Before it breaks down into compost, mulch offers the following benefits:

- Weed control
- Water retention and root cooling
- Soilborne disease control
- Soil erosion control
- Soil conditioning

In the following sections we'll look deeper into each of these benefits.

Weed Control

All mulches excel as weed barriers. They block the light from getting through to the soil, making it difficult for weed seeds to germinate. And they tend to smother any little weeds that do manage to emerge. Those few hardy weeds that rear their little necks out of the mulch will tend to be weakly attached to the ground, making them very easy to pull out.

Digging Deeper

Mulching is yet another great way to use the materials you have around your yard and home that would otherwise end up in the landfills. For me, these practices are first class as far as recycling. My advice is to mulch every spot of bare soil in your yard. The transformation in your yard will astound you.

Water Retention

Gardeners always welcome ways to outsmart evaporation. A favorite benefit of mulching is water retention. Compost is excellent at retaining moisture. General mulching keeps the soil shielded from the sun, which cuts down on evaporation. Slower evaporation means the need for less water, which saves both time and money.

Root Protection

Mulch helps reduce the fluctuation of temperatures in the soil. Rapid temperature fluctuations can be harmful to plants' root systems. By holding in moisture, the roots of your plants will stay cool during the hot months, as well.

Soilborne Disease Barrier

When a plant contracts a disease and its leaves fall on the ground, often the disease lives on those leaves waiting to infect another host. A prime example is bacteria leaf blight, which attacks tomato plants.

If your tomatoes had leaf blight last year, the infected leaves probably fell to the ground. Those infected leaves are now in the soil, slowly decomposing, and the blight is lying in wait for a new victim. Now, suppose you plant new tomatoes in the same place that the old ones were growing last season.

You water the tomatoes, and water hits the ground and splashes some of the bacteria back up onto the leaves of the new plants. The disease cycle starts over again. It works the same way with other diseases that live in the soil.

However, by spreading 1 to 3 inches of mulch around the plants and throughout the bed, it will act as a barrier between any contaminated leaves or soil. Use this trick for strawberry plants to help keep botrytis at bay.

Mulch Prevents Soil Erosion

Nothing is more frustrating to gardeners than seeing their gorgeous compost wash away with the winter rains and wind. If you cover your bare soil with mulch, you'll get to hang on to what you worked for.

 **Prickly Problem**

Soil sediment is the biggest pollutant in our waterways. Because mulching helps prevent soil erosion, it's a very eco-friendly activity.

def•i•ni•tion

Tilth describes the physical structure of soil as it influences plant growth. When a soil has good tilth it is porous, allowing water to infiltrate easily and permitting roots to grow without obstruction.

Soil Conditioner

Mulches not only become compost and therefore add nutritional value to the soil, but they also support helpful life forms within the soil. The addition of organic matter supports and encourages earthworm activity. Worms improve the *tilth* of the soil by aerating it and adding nutrients of their own.

How to Use Mulch

When you add mulch specifically for weed control, you'll want to be sure that all the weeds are removed in that area first. When you spread the layer of mulch, don't skimp. In a sunny area, you'll want to use 4 to 6 inches of mulch. You may only need a 2- to 3-inch-thick layer in the shade. Use what the bed looked like before you mulched as a guide. If there were a lot of weeds growing in that area, then you know they do well there and you should add a thicker layer of mulch. If there were only a few weeds, you can get away with less.

Avoid placing the mulch up against the base of plants and the trunks of trees. Mulch really belongs from the drip line of the plant and outward. I have to admit, I do go a little bit in from the drip line because it make me feel like I'm making plant roots all nice and cozy, but be careful not to get too close. Shoot for creating a "doughnut" of mulch around the plant as opposed to "volcano" of mulch mounded up around its stem or trunk.

Another thing to consider when spreading mulch is how much "settling" there will be. Ideally, you want the mulch, when settled, to be about 4 inches thick. You want oxygen to be able to reach the soil, and going much thicker than 6 inches is going to make it unlikely for that to happen.

Prickly Problem

When mulch is piled high on tree trunks, fungal diseases find it easy to move in and take hold. It encourages rotting, plus rodents think it makes a cool fort and might set up home there.

Some mulches settle more than others. Leaves and straw are far more likely to settle than wood chips, for example. So go ahead and pile leaves and straw on at about 6–8 inches high because they'll end up around half of that in a couple of days. If you're using wood chips, then spread only 3–4 inches because those guys aren't settling.

Think doughnut, not volcano, when mulching around trees and plants.

The Best Time to Mulch

Personally, I mulch whenever I feel like it because I hate weeding. But most garden-ers would say that the optimal time for mulching is during the fall, winter, and early spring. Your plants are most likely to freeze to death from bitter cold and snow during the fall and winter, and that's also when soil erosion is at its peak due to the rain. In the spring, ideally you want to mulch before the weeds start shooting up.

Prickly Problem _____

One concern for gardeners is that plant pests like snails and earwigs can hide in mulch and launch a sneak-attack on the fresh growth on plants. By not mulching all the way up to the base of the plants, you won't be giving those critters a safe route from the mulch to your plants.

Which Organic Mulch?

Some organic materials make better sense than others for specific areas. Before you add mulch, consider the type of garden bed you're mulching. The following sections list the various options available.

Grass Clippings

The average homeowner overlooks the many benefits of grass clippings. You already know how great they are for the compost bin and grasscycling. But clippings are terrific as mulch, too. While you can use them anywhere you'd lay mulch, the foundation plantings (landscaping) around your home may not be the best place simply because grass clippings aren't as attractive as other mulches for shrub borders.

The optimal place to use grass-clipping mulch is around vegetables like tomatoes. Grass has a tremendous amount of nitrogen to burn. So when you put the clippings around tomato plants, it warms the soil up—which gets the plants on their way to production. Not to mention all the nitrogen that's released into the soil as they break down.

The trick with grass clippings is to keep the layer under 4 inches thick, because if it's piled much higher, the grass will mat and become oxygen-deprived, which will lead to bad odors. Don't let this tip scare you off, though; grass clippings are an extremely useful resource.

Wood Chips or Shredded Bark

Wood chips and shredded bark are probably the most widely used materials for mulch anywhere—and for good reason. They make excellent mulches due to the fact that they are heavy enough to stay put and don't need to be replaced very often as they decompose slowly. They're terrific for water retention, and they're attractive in landscaping.

They come in different textures, sizes, and colors from which to choose. This also makes them popular with homeowners. The only drawback would be the fact that they can take some nitrogen from the soil while they decompose.

Digging Deeper

Wood chips make great mulch, but they come with a potential problem: while the chips are slowly decomposing, they tend to rob the soil of nitrogen, which means there may be less of that nutrient available to your plants. To avoid this problem and make the most of your wood chips, first spread a 2- to 3-inch layer of compost around the plants or throughout the landscape area. Then put a 2-inch layer of wood chips down over the top of the compost. Not only does this add two mulching sources to protect and amend your soil, but the compost counteracts the nitrogen-hogging carbon in the wood chips.

Compost

Compost from your compost bin is probably the ultimate in mulches. Not only does it have every capability that other mulches do, but it's already loaded with turbo nutrients that leach into the soil immediately as well as disease-fighting properties.

Prickly Problem

Are weevils threatening to take over your rhododendrons? Mulch around them with 3 inches of cedar chips to ward off these little pests. Add fresh chips each year.

Dry Leaves

Gather as many dry leaves as you can in the fall. You can use the leaves immediately on your harvested vegetable bed by turning them under the soil and letting them break down over the winter. Come spring, you'll have a nice humusy soil to work with.

Alternately, you can save the leaves until you plant the vegetable garden and use them as mulch during the growing season. After the harvest, turn them under.

Newspaper or Cardboard

Newspaper is the ultimate in mulches. Most people already have a lot of it on hand, and if they don't, their neighbor probably does. It's completely biodegradable, and the good critters in the soil love it. You can use it everywhere: in your garden and beds as mulch, in your compost pile as a carbon source, and in your worm bins as bedding.

While it can certainly be used as mulch by itself, newspaper gives everything else a helping hand when you lay it underneath another mulch. If you use it in your landscaping, you can cover it with lovely colored wood chips or shredded bark.

When using it as mulch, add around five layers, depending on how much you have on hand. Newspaper decomposes pretty quickly, so adding a few more layers doesn't hurt. If the wind is blowing it around while you're trying to spread it out, just dampen the paper with some water.

Cardboard works exactly the same way as newspaper, but it'll last longer. I prefer to use the cardboard in walkways or over entire beds like in a compost sandwich rather than in between my plant crops. Newspaper is easier to work with when you're placing it between individual plants.

Pine Needles

Many people living in the woods have an abundance of pine needles available to them. They can make excellent mulch, but here's the deal: use it under the trees they came from or use it in a bed of plants that loves acidity such as azaleas or rhododendrons. Pine needles are loaded with acid, and if you're not careful, you'll damage plants that can't tolerate a low soil pH.

Straw or Seedless Hay

Both straw and hay (seedless) work well as mulch, although you probably don't want to use it around landscape plantings simply because it's not very attractive. Also, if you use thin layers of either one, they tend to blow away easily.

Some of the best places to use straw and hay are in vegetable beds and the paths between the rows. In the pathways, not only do they suppress weeds well, but they keep your feet out of the wet soil or mud.

Living Mulch

Certain plants serve as living mulches that can be planted among food crops or while the garden bed is at rest for the season. These plants not only control soil erosion, but add nutrients like nitrogen back into soils that have been depleted by crops (such as corn) that are heavy feeders. They're so special that we devote Chapter 14 to them.

Wise Worm _____

When you're purchasing bagged mulch, be aware that some mulches may contain hazardous material like arsenic from pressure-treated wood. Gardeners can purchase safe mulch that's guaranteed free of any unacceptable material by looking for the Mulch and Soil Council's certification logo on the bag. To learn more about certified safe mulch and soil go to www.mulchandsoilcouncil.org.

Use What You've Got

When it comes to mulches, use what's readily available. Tree and shrub prunings are perfect for using in a border. They could be shredded for ultimate versatility, but they don't have to be.

How about that old Christmas tree? If you have no way of shredding the entire tree, just cut off some branches and lay the entire branch under shrubs as mulch.

Maybe you have a huge stack of newspapers that you haven't sent to be recycled yet. Well, recycle them in your compost, gardens, and as mulch instead.

And don't forget to look in your compost pile or bin for the ultimate mulch.

Inorganic Materials as Mulch

While rocks, pebbles, sand, and granite are certainly natural products, they aren't organic. That is, they didn't come from what used to be a living thing and they will not decompose and contribute nutrients to the soil.

But there's nothing wrong with using inorganic matter as mulch; in fact, if that's what you have to work with, by all means use it. You are recycling a material that would otherwise be thrown away, while preventing soil erosion and conserving water.

Other inorganic materials that are also "unnatural" are also effective mulches for the garden or landscape. These include man-made glass, black plastic, and landscape fabric.

The Least You Need to Know

- Mulch is excellent for weed control, water retention, root protection, soilborne diseases, erosion, and soil conditioning.

- Fall, winter, and early spring are optimal times to mulch. However, any day is a good day to mulch.

- Compost is the ultimate mulching material you can use. Plus, you can use it under any other type of mulch.

- Organic materials are different than natural materials in that not every natural material once came from a living plant or animal.

- Look for materials you already have on hand to use as mulch.

Chapter 14

Plant Your Compost: Green Manures and Cover Crops

In This Chapter

◆ Living mulches

◆ Green manures vs. cover crops

◆ Legumes, grasses, and cereals

◆ Knocking down, tilling, and turning under

Cover crops and green manures are directly in line with compost bins, vermicomposting, grasscycling, and even mulch—they're all a form of composting. In other words, they're all about turning natural resources back into plant and animal nutrition.

The term "living mulch" labels several categories of gardening practices. Although the terms "green manures" and "cover crops" are often used interchangeably, they do have slightly different meanings. Both are considered forms of composting, as the plants in each category perform many of the same functions that traditional composting does—and then some.

Both types of living mulches are eventually turned under the soil and, as they deteriorate, they release their nutrition into the soil. In this chapter you will read about several you can use to take advantage of this unique composting style.

A "green manure" is a crop planted in a garden bed while the main vegetable crops are on hiatus. Green manures are sown after the main crop is harvested and then turned under while they're still green. They add nutrients (predominately nitrogen) back into the soil that the previous food crop has used up, increasing the soil's fertility for the next season's vegetables.

The primary purpose behind planting "cover crops" is for erosion control and to block weed growth. However, cover crops can perform double-duty by improving the soil's organic matter, as well. Cover crops are usually planted at the same general time as green manures and are also tilled under while they're still green.

Occasionally, both green manures and cover crops are planted along side primary crops to attract beneficial insects for pollination.

Living Mulch

Living mulch is a term used loosely in the gardening world to refer to anything from ground cover to plants meant to offer the soil nutrition (green manures), and those that are planted to keep erosion and weeds at bay (cover crops).

All living mulches are widely used to rejuvenate soil that's been overplanted or has had crops, such as corn, that draw heavily on the soil for their nutrition.

Once your summer crops are harvested, you can literally plant nutritional goods back into the garden bed and improve the soil. When you plant green manures in the fall, they act as a cover crop and keep your soil in the bed where you want it. They also smother and crowd out early spring weeds.

Both cover crops and green manures are typically grown in areas where food crops are planted. This is because you wouldn't normally risk disturbing perennial roots or flower gardens by turning another crop under where there are permanent plants.

That said, many fruit tree growers plant green manures like clover or vetch between their rows of trees to encourage beneficial predatory insects. Cover crops are also routinely used along with grape vines.

Living Mulches Protect and Add to Soil Structure

Cover crops and green manures help soil structure by loosening the earth in heavy, clay soils down by the crop's roots. They also reduce erosion by hanging fast to the soil during winter rains. Some of them also "fix" the nitrogen in the soil so you don't lose the precious nutrient. After they're tilled under, these plants add organic matter to your soil, which is the whole point of composting in the first place.

Deep-rooted green manures such as alfalfa draw nitrogen deeper into the soil. Legumes in general collect nitrogen from the air and store it in their roots, releasing it once the legume crop gets cut and dies. All cover crops, once they're turned over, add organic matter to the soil.

Green Manures Crowd Out Weeds

Any cover crop you plant is going to help crowd out or smother weeds, which is a time- and back-saver for the gardener. But some of these crops perform this feat particularly well. Buckwheat and rapeseed are both examples of cover crops that perform stellar weed control.

Choosing Your Cover Crop or Green Manure

Many seed catalogs, and agricultural suppliers have green manures and cover crop seed available. But before you start ear-marking catalogs or actually buying cover crop seeds, you should take some time to answer the following questions, which will help guide you to make the best choices for your situation.

What is your USDA hardiness zone? Find out which crops will thrive in your area. For instance, ryes and clovers are hardy enough to tough out winter weather, whereas fenugreek and buckwheat won't survive hard frosts.

If you have a general sense of your hardiness zone but want some intimate insight, call your local university cooperative extension office. They have their finger on the pulse of these things. This zone map isn't perfect, considering how many microclimates we all have, but it's fairly accurate and the best place to start.

What's your primary goal for planting a cover crop? Are you interested in simply adding nutrients to the soil? You'll have a wide variety of choices in this case. Did you grow a heavy feeder like corn and want to provide some turbo nitrogen? Legumes offer nitrogen in spades. Does your garden area become invaded by weeds, and you're mainly looking for some control over them? If so, then buckwheat may be right for you.

Which season are you planting your cover crop? Do you want to plant in the early fall while the vegetable bed is at rest for months? Maybe you're interested in planting a green manure in the summer in between crops and you'll need a fast grower. Let your seed source know when you'll be planting so they can help you choose the right seed.

What was planted in the garden bed before the cover crop? Just like vegetables, you want to avoid planting crops from the same family in the same space back to back. To avoid rolling out the red carpet for plant pests, it's best to rotate between crop families.

If you had cabbage or broccoli in the bed, you may want to plant a legume instead of mustard, because mustard is in the *brassica* family with broccoli. If the previous crop was peas, plant something other than a green manure from the legume family.

Take your answers to these questions with you when you place an order for cover crops or green manures. The company you'll be dealing with should be knowledgeable about their products and their needs. They'll be able to guide you toward an appropriate selection purchase for your situation. Let them help you.

Wise Worm

Inoculate is an inexpensive dusting of beneficial bacteria. Legumes work their magic best when they're inoculated before they're planted. This puts the correct bacteria directly into the root zone, which ensures that the crop has better growth, not to mention holds more nitrogen.

Some argue that it's a waste of time to inoculate if the cover crop is planted in a biologically active area that has benefited from previous composting practices. However, because inoculating is so inexpensive, it's probably safer to go ahead and use it even if you've composted in the area before.

Legumes: Nitrogen, Anyone?

Legumes are a green manure that brings a little something extra to garden soil in the form of a mega-dose of nitrogen. Bacteria live in the roots of legume plants and "fix" or gather and hold nitrogen in their root system. They end up fixing more nitrogen than they need for themselves and, after they die, they release a large amount of nitrogen into the soil. This is like giving a triple-shot of latte to your soil and therefore your veggies.

Alfalfa (*Medicago sativa*)

Alfalfa is usually a perennial legume, although some annual varieties are available. In many zones you can get two crops out of it for the season. Alfalfa likes to be planted in a rich soil with a neutral pH.

- ◆ Sow it in the spring at a rate of 1 to 2 pounds per 1,000 square feet.

- ◆ Plant seeds in the spring or late summer and then cover shallowly with topsoil. *Broadcasting* alfalfa seeds in the spring is preferable because the soil stays uniformly moist.

- ◆ Inoculate the area before planting the alfalfa if you haven't grown it in that bed before.

- ◆ Alfalfa is slow to establish itself.

- ◆ Annual alfalfa will grow during the fall months and then die in the winter. But the perennial varieties will go dormant for the winter unless waterlogged and then frozen.

- ◆ It doesn't grow well in extremely compacted soils; it likes soil it can sink its roots into.

- ◆ It likes a neutral soil pH the best, and will tolerate higher alkaline levels but resents high acidity.

- ◆ This legume attracts slugs, so if you live in an area that's prone to the slimy guys, you may want to keep iron phosphate (often sold as "Sluggo") on hand to battle them.

- ◆ Once alfalfa is established, it makes an excellent cover crop and improves soil structure by adding biomass as well as helping to break up compacted soils.

def•i•ni•tion

Broadcasting is the process of spreading seeds, soil, or a plant amendment like fertilizer evenly across any given area. In smaller areas this is done with a random motion by hand or a hand-held spreading tool.

Digging Deeper

If you're growing alfalfa, you might consider cutting or mowing the first pass of growth and tossing it into your compost pile as an excellent "green." After the alfalfa grows a couple more feet, turn it into the garden bed. You get two cool uses for the price of one planting.

Red Clover (*Trifolium pratense*)

Red clover is a legume that's a biennial or short-lived perennial. Once established, it's an excellent protection against soil erosion.

- Broadcast it over an area at a rate of 4 to 8 ounces per 1,000 square feet; less if planted with a forage.

- It needs to have its seeds inoculated with Rhizobium trifolii and planted shallow.

- Red clover likes cool conditions and moist soil. It does best in a soil pH of 6.0–7.0 (slightly acidic) and tolerates shade.

- This is a slow-starter, but not as slow as alfalfa.

- It over-winters well and flowers about 65 days after it's sowed; it reblooms about every 30 to 35 days thereafter.

- This legume is a good nitrogen-fixer and adds good biomass to the soil.

- It improves soil conditions, which encourages microbial life as well as adds structural strength.

- It improves the water-holding capacity of soil.

Hairy Vetch (*Vicia villosa*)

Be careful not to confuse hairy vetch with its cousin crown vetch (*Coronilla varia*), which is an aggressive variety that you don't want in your garden.

- Hairy vetch is an annual winter legume with a shallow root system.

- Its seeds require an inoculant before planting and should be planted in late summer or fall, but do best when in the ground by mid-August.

- Broadcast seeds at the rate of 1 to 2 pounds per 1,000 square feet.

- It grows best in sandy soils with a pH of 6.0–7.0 and is drought-tolerant once the plants are established.

- It fixes so much nitrogen that it's possible for the cover crop to provide all of the next crop's nitrogen requirements for the season.

- It tolerates extremely cold temperatures and therefore it over-winters well.

- Hairy vetch has a vinelike growth habit and is often sown with rye.

- It has blue-violet blossoms, supports many beneficial insects, and adds to the biodiversity of the soil.

- It provides good erosion control and weed suppression once the plants are established.

Field Peas or Austrian Winter Peas (*Pisum sativum*)

Field pea is an annual winter legume ideal for planting in colder climates, as it takes some freezing temperatures in stride.

- Sow it in late summer to early fall at the rate of 2 to 5 ounces per 1,000 square feet.

- It germinates well in moist soil but with good drainage.

- It has shallow roots and thrives in loamy or even clay soils, but resents sandy soils.

- As a vine-type plant, the weak stems tend to lie down. If you want the plants to stand up, you need to grow a second crop along with it like rye or oats.

- It is not a drought-tolerant crop; it's necessary to water evenly.

- It flowers in white, pink, and purple.

- It doesn't provide good weed control.

- It fixes nitrogen in the soil at the high rate of 100 pounds per acre.

- It breaks down easily and adds good biomass to the soil.

- Pests such as nematodes and aphids are attracted by it; however, it also provides good cover for beneficial insects.

Sweet Clover (*Melilotus spp.*)

These legumes come in both annual and perennial varieties. Sweet clover is also said to bring phosphorous and potassium to the root zone as well as nitrogen.

- Its seeds should be inoculated and may need to be *scarified* before planting.

def•i•ni•tion

Scarified seeds refer to seeds that have been nicked or scraped on a rough surface such as sandpaper or a nail file. Gardeners scarify hard-shelled seeds in order to encourage germination.

- Plant it in early spring and cover lightly with soil.

- It is often under-seeded where corn is planted.

- Most clovers are quite winter-hardy and are capable of penetrating clay soils.

- It flowers anywhere from May to September depending on the variety.

- Clovers can be grown in a wide variety of soils and most despise acidic soils and poor drainage.

- It readily attracts beneficial insects and has a strong taproot that may help hard-pan soils.

- Like the other legumes, clovers are excellent for fixing nitrogen.

Soybeans (*Glycine max*)

This annual legume will germinate in no time at all if you give it a warm and moist soil.

- The seeds should be inoculated and planted in the spring or summer months.

- Broadcast 2 to 3 pounds per 1,000 square feet. Sow these guys thickly and you'll be rewarded with fast cover.

- Seeds tend to quickly cover the ground, but the plants tend to stay short.

- Soybeans will tolerate poor drainage. They grow well in a wide range of soils unless it's extremely dry or overly saturated.

- They're cold-tender, don't handle frost well, and they break down quickly once cut down.

Nonlegumes Work, Too

Green manures usually fall into two categories: legumes and everything else. Everything else refers to grains and grasses. Grains and grasses like winter rye, rape, wheat, and oats basically work well as cover crops for erosion control and add biomass or organic matter. Mustard is often grown as a green manure for its protective properties against nematodes and *verticillium wilt*.

Oats (*Avena sativa*)

Oat is a fast-growing annual grass that pairs well with clovers. Oats are used as forage, grain, as well as a cover crop.

- ◆ Plant oat in the spring or summer in a moist soil. It prefers a well-drained, loamy situation and grows best if watered regularly.

- ◆ It prefers moist, cool conditions, but are killed by cold winter weather.

- ◆ Oat will tolerate a wide range of soil pH but prefers the soil to be a bit sweet.

- ◆ If conditions become too hot and dry, the oats won't cover well and will perform poorly as far as erosion and weed control.

- ◆ Oat effectively smothers weeds when established.

- ◆ Oat offers high biomass to soils and releases nitrogen, although not as much as rye.

Mustard (*Brassica spp.*)

You'll often see mustard growing between grapevine rows to crowd out weeds while adding nutrients to the crop's soil.

- ◆ Mustards seed should be planted in late summer (mid-August) on an evenly firm seedbed about ½ inch deep.

- ◆ It enjoys a neutral pH and a moist, well-drained soil.

- ◆ Mustard is usually grown for a short six weeks as a cover crop.

- ◆ Seedlings emerge five to ten days after sowing and will cover the ground in four to five weeks. Flowers bloom at about six weeks.

- ◆ Mustard has shown reasonable suppression of some pathogens such as verticillium on potato plants; fusarium in carrots; and Pythium, Fusarium, and Rhizoctonia root rots in beans.

- ◆ Mustard won't survive once a hard frost hits, so it can be planted with a rye in order to cover the soil through the winter.

♦ Although the seedlings have a hard time competing with weeds, mustard is successful at smothering weeds for the following crop (once established).

♦ Mustard adds good organic matter and breaks up hardpan soils.

Rapeseed (*Brassica napus*)

Rapeseed is also known as Canola and summer turnip. It's a winter or spring annual that belongs to the mustard, cabbage, and broccoli family.

♦ Plant seeds between mid-August to mid-September. Before the cold weather begins, the plants will have reached the stage of six to eight leaves and will be considered established.

♦ Rapeseed will tolerate a wide variety of soils and soil pHs. However, it resists poorly drained soils, especially when trying to become established.

♦ It tends to gather nitrogen during the fall while it's actively growing.

♦ It makes a stable groundcover over winter for erosion, and its roots help loosen hardpan soils, thereby improving tilth.

♦ Rapeseed is a good source of biomass for the soil and does an excellent job smothering weeds.

♦ It's highly drought-tolerant and not winter-hardy.

♦ Mow or chop down plants during their spring bloom and turn under the soil.

Buckwheat (*Fagopyrum esculentum*)

If you tend to have a weed problem in your garden bed, buckwheat is top of the line for crowding out and smothering weeds. Buckwheat more than holds its own against even the most invasive plants. It's also one of the fastest ways to build up your garden soil in a hurry. It has sweet-smelling flowers that attract bees to help pollinate anything around it.

♦ Plant buckwheat seeds in the late spring or summer at the rate of 2 to 3 pounds per 1,000 square feet well after the last frost date and at least four weeks before the first fall frost.

♦ Buckwheat is a broadleaf summer annual.

◆ It emerges three to five days after sowing seeds.

◆ It's the fastest-growing cover crop around and flowers in 4 to 6 weeks to quickly set seed in 10 to 12 weeks.

◆ Buckwheat is cold-sensitive; cold temperatures and frost kill it quickly.

◆ It enjoys a wide range of soil types but performs its best in a well-drained soil with a pH range of 5.0 to 7.0. Buckwheat tolerates infertile, wet, compacted, and droughty soils.

◆ Buckwheat is excellent at pushing out or smothering even the most invasive weeds.

◆ Organic farmers often use buckwheat to extract extra phosphorus from the soil.

◆ It attracts beneficial insects such as honeybees.

◆ Buckwheat composts easily.

Prickly Problem

Buckwheat can have mature seeds while the plant is still flowering. To avoid the possibility of it reseeding itself when you turn it under, be careful to turn it under on the earlier side (7 to 10 days before flowering is optimal).

Winter or Cereal Rye (*Secale cereale*)

Winter rye is popular as a grain, forage, and a cover crop. Don't confuse winter rye (*Secale cereale*) with ryegrass (*Lolium mutiflorum*). They're not the same species and they perform differently.

◆ Plant rye in early fall after your primary food crop harvest. It can also be seeded in the early spring despite the frost.

◆ Broadcast seeds in late summer or fall at a rate of 2 to 3 pounds per 1,000 square feet of land.

◆ This annual prefers well-drained soil but will tolerate all soil types.

◆ Winter rye is extremely cold-tolerant and disease resistant.

◆ It's quite adept at gathering nitrogen and grows faster than most other winter cereals such as barley and wheat.

◆ Winter rye is known for its erosion control and soil-building properties.

◆ As a forage crop, it is harvested for baling in May, but can be used for grazing in the fall or spring.

◆ Due to winter rye's rapid growth, it's a cover crop that can be harvested early, making it possible to get a double harvest.

◆ Rye is terrific at building soil structure; however, it can sometimes suppress other seeds from germinating. So the best way to work with rye as a cover crop is to plant your food crop's seeds after the rye has been tilled under for a few weeks.

Annual Ryegrass (*Lolium multiflorum*)

Annual ryegrass is also known as Italian ryegrass. It is a very competitive annual winter grass, meaning that its seedlings have no trouble establishing themselves quickly. Don't confuse annual ryegrass with winter rye (*Secale cereale*), which is an entirely different crop.

◆ Both annual and perennial ryegrass are bunch grasses. Italian (annual) ryegrass grows best in temperate climates.

◆ Ryegrass tolerates a variety of soil situations but is particularly suited for clay or silty soils with a neutral pH.

◆ Annual ryegrass tolerates temporary flooding and extended wet periods, but it doesn't do well in the shade.

◆ Because it's a rapid grower, ryegrass covers land quickly and is therefore a perfect temporary pasture.

◆ This is another versatile grass that can be used for grazing in the fall or spring, baled, and used as a green manure or cover crop.

◆ It's often mixed with an annual legume for extra performance.

◆ Ryegrass seed is fairly inexpensive and requires no inoculants.

◆ Careful and repeated mowing practices are required to keep the rye in check if grown with grapevines, as the rye could compete with the grape crop.

French Marigolds (*Tagetes patula*)

This has to be the sunniest cover crop anywhere. Use marigolds as cover crop between your rows of vegetables while they're actively growing. Although, you could certainly cover an entire bed with the little ladies and turn them under just as you would any cover crop or green manure.

♦ Marigolds are annuals that bloom in the summer and fall.

♦ They are extremely easy to germinate and grow at a moderate rate.

♦ Tagetes doesn't winter-over, so you don't have to knock this cover crop down unless you don't want it to reseed at all. Then treat it like any other crop and turn under right before or just after blooming.

♦ Broadcast or plant in rows, packing a light soil over them.

♦ Marigolds suppress nematodes in the root zone.

♦ Marigold seeds can be more expensive than other cover crops.

Wise Worm

Take advantage of the tall weeds that have grown in your garden bed during the down months and use them as a green manure! There are only two things to keep in mind if you use this method. First, be sure to knock them all the way down before they go to seed. Second, be sure that the weed that's growing in the bed isn't one that will regrow from perennial roots or rhizomes. Nothing is easier or more satisfying than putting weeds to work for you.

Mix It Up

Can't decide which cover crop to plant? Why not plant several green manures at once in the same place? This allows the soil to receive a variety of nutrition, giving it balance. Planting a variety of legumes, grasses, or grains gives the soil nutritional variety. The grasses and grains provide fiber and organic matter more quickly than the legumes, and the legumes give the soil that turbo charge of nitrogen.

The following general cover-crop blend is perfect for improving the soil in your garden. One of the perks of planting with a mix is that the plants bloom at different intervals, attracting beneficial insects for a longer period of time. This blend comes from Peaceful Valley Garden in Grass Valley, California, where they sell these seeds as a mix.

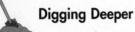

40 percent Bell Beans

20 percent Magnus or BioMaster Winter Peas

15 percent Lana Vetch

15 percent Purple Vetch

10 percent Cayuse Oats

You'll need approximately 3 to 5 pounds of seed per 1,000 square feet of garden space. For a cold winter-zone cover-crop mix, try the following "recipe":

85 percent Hairy Vetch

15 percent Cereal Rye

You'll need approximately 2 to 3 pounds of seeds per 1,000 square feet of garden area. This blend is useful where winters reach -20°F.

Putting All That Goodness Back into the Soil

If you're planting your cover crop in the fall, you may want to plant a crop like winter rye that can take the cold weather in stride. In the spring, cut down the rye and turn it under the soil. You can also wait until just after the plants bloom, as it calls in all kinds of beneficial insects.

Don't wait too long, though, because you don't want the cover crop going to seed in the garden before you knock it down.

You can use a weed trimmer or your basic spade shovel to knock down as well as turn the cover crop. The idea is to knock it down permanently so that it dies and adds organic matter, and, in the case of the legumes, releases the nitrogen from its roots into the soil.

By "tilling" or "turning under," you don't need to rent a power tiller or even use a hand tiller. All you need is a spade shovel and a little elbow grease and turn the plants into the soil with the shovel. You don't need to completely hide every piece of green under the soil—just get it in there so that the plants are held in place. You want the plants to be just under the earth so they can break down and add organic matter to your soil.

If you're planting the green manure in the spring and are using a legume crop, turn them over just before they begin to bloom. In both cases, you'll want to wait two to four weeks before planting a food crop to make the most of your cover crops.

Digging Deeper

Do you dread the idea of turning anything over? Here are a couple of alternatives for you:

When it's time to turn the cover crop over, sandwich it instead. Cover the entire area with thick layers of wet newspaper or cardboard. Then spread a compost layer over the whole garden bed. The crops will die and decompose into the soil like they should and you've added even more organic materials to the bed.

Another trick is to deliberately plant a tender crop that can't tolerate the heavy frost or snow. Start it in the late summer or early fall and let it grow until a frost comes along and kills it for you. This is the epitome of armchair gardening.

The Least You Need to Know

♦ Green manures are crops that are turned under while they're still green. They're grown predominately to feed the soil extra nutrients such as nitrogen.

♦ Cover crops are predominately grown for erosion control and to block weak growth. They are often tilled under the soil to add organic matter and nutrients to the soil, just like green manures.

♦ Green manures and cover crops are both considered living mulches.

♦ Both green manures and cover crops help with erosion, water retention, and weed suppression; add organic matter and nutrients; and encourage beneficial insects.

♦ Many cover crops are sown as a mix to take advantage of the best properties offered by individual crops.

Chapter 15

Composting as a Community

In This Chapter

- ◆ How you can compost as a neighborhood
- ◆ Community garden composting piles
- ◆ Drawing on local government resources
- ◆ Inspiring stories

Now that you know all the benefits of composting on a personal level, it's time to consider taking it to a whole new level: your community.

Start a Compost Rotation in Your Neighborhood

Starting a neighborhood compost rotation is not only a great way to introduce neighbors to composting, but it gives the entire community a reason to support something together other than a crime watch. This type of composting makes it possible for everyone to participate by contributing their week's worth of compostable materials to a new compost pile each week. In just a few weeks, your neighborhood should be able to begin harvesting their community garden gold on an ongoing basis.

Begin by hosting a small get-together in which someone gives a presentation or plays a video on composting techniques so that every neighbor has an idea of how composting works.

Digging Deeper

The idea of starting a neighborhood compost rotation comes from Janelle Orsi and Emily Doskow's book, *The Sharing Solution: How to Save Money, Simplify Your Life & Build Community* (Nolo, 2009).

Wise Worm

Composting as a neighborhood opens up the possibility of jump-starting other neighborhood get-togethers. When neighborhoods can see the positive difference they can make in their own neighborhoods, it trickles on to the entire community.

All the neighbors who plan to participate in the program need to build or acquire their own compost bin. Everyone involved collects organic materials in a garbage can for the week. At the end of the week, each neighbor brings his or her garbage can to a designated neighbor's bin. This first bin is filled with all of the compostable items from everyone's can that first week.

After one neighbor's bin is filled, the participants add their organic material to the next neighbor's bin, and so on until every bin is filled. Each family tends to their own compost pile, turning it and keeping it moist and aerated, until the compost is done. Usually the first bin that was filled is ready for harvesting first.

At that point, all the neighbors bring a wheelbarrow to the finished compost bin and gather compost for their garden beds or yards. Continue this process until all the compost is harvested.

If you don't know very many of your neighbors, ease them into the idea. First, start a compost pile at your own home and invite neighbors to share in your bounty. Once they get to know you better and begin to recognize the benefits of composting, you can begin discussing the possibility of creating a community composting network.

Composting at Your Community Gardens

Another way to compost as a community is at your community gardens, as many of them already have open composting bins going. Instead of creating a composting co-op on your street, city residents are encouraged to collect their compostables in a garbage can and bring the organic waste to the local community gardens site, where the compost pile is constructed.

If compost bins are already located at your community gardens, call your city and find out who is in charge of the gardens. Explain that you want to encourage people to compost and ask permission to use the compost bins at the gardens. If they don't already have bins constructed, ask if you can arrange to have a group of neighbors build some.

Once you are granted permission, prepare fliers explaining the community composting project—and don't forget to include a list of compostable items on the flier. Distribute the fliers to as many neighboring homes as you can. Pin up posters at local coffeehouses, supermarkets, parks, and your community center.

When the compost is ready to use, bring a big bag to the community compost bins and stock up on garden gold for your own garden.

Your Helpful County

Most counties are very interested in helping their residents adopt composting practices. Counties have been known to host "composting awareness weeks," and some even go so far as to give county residents composting bins or sell them at a significant discount as long as they're shipped to an address within their county.

Your county may offer composting and vermicomposting workshops, many of which are free to residents. They may also offer composting sessions geared toward community groups and school-age children.

Start your county composting research through your local university cooperative extension office, county offices, or extension or county websites.

> **Wise Worm**
>
> Ask your county about any working compost bins that you can visit. These are usually set up at public gardens where you can peruse the plantings and make an afternoon of it. If your neighborhood rotation project finds itself with an overabundance of compost, the community garden will probably be thrilled to receive it.

Kudos to Composting Companies

Many companies are committed to disposing of their products in an environmentally friendly fashion—and more and more, this involves composting. Not only do they deserve a shout-out here, but they can be used to spark creative composting ideas for others:

Fiberactive Organics, LLC in Raleigh, North Carolina (www.fiberactiveorganics. com) makes table linens and other products from organic cotton fabrics. Julie Mullin and her employees place their cotton fabrics and pieces of paper into their rabbitry and chicken nests, where they are covered in manure. Then the organic matter goes either into the compost pile, the compost bin, or under the rabbit cages for the worms.

Under the hutches the cotton helps absorb urine and feces. If maggots appear under her rabbit hutches, she brings the chickens in to have a feast. At this point, everything is nearly decomposed, but Julie will toss it into the compost bin where the manure and urine on the fabric can really heat things up. Her compost goes to a community garden that she organized for her Vietnam refugee seamstresses and their families.

Jack's Harvest in Atlanta, Georgia (www.jacksharvest.com) is a frozen organic baby food company that composts all of their fruit and vegetable peels. Heather, the owner of Jack's Harvest, takes all the peels home with her, composts them, and uses the compost in her garden.

Coffee Break Cafe in Massachusetts (www.coffeebreakcafe.net) is a small chain of coffee shops that started composting last year. Between recycling and composting they have decreased the amount of trash they send to the landfill by at least half.

ASK Apparel in Nashville Tennessee (www.askapparel.com) composts much of their waste material from their production process. They're an eco-dye shop, using natural dyes such as woods, flowers, and clays to impart sustainable color onto cloth. They in turn use this compost for their small farm; one of several regional suppliers of their natural dye pigment.

Taco Del Mar (www.tacodelmar.com), a quick-service Mexican restaurant chain, collaborated with Trellis Earth, a Portland-based company, to create a new line-up of green, eco-friendly packaging. Now, a year later, the packaging has rolled into over 180 stores in Washington, Oregon, and Canada.

These products range from utensils to carry-out bags, plates to garbage bags. Taco Del Mar's 16-piece line-up is made of Trellis Earth's PLA resin, composed of corn and vegetable starch, and biodegradable polymers, making each piece biodegradable in commercial landfills.

Over a 12-month period Taco Del Mar reduced its plastic output by over 300,000 pounds (equal to over 169 tons of plastic waste), and reduced the use of fossil fuel by almost 1,000,000 pounds. This equals planting over 20,000 trees!

Atlas Paper Mills in Miami, Florida (www.atlaspapermills.com) is a leader in the production of paper products, including bathroom toilet paper and paper-towel rolls, using 100 percent recycled fiber, and a manufacturing process free of chlorine, chlorine derivatives, or any other potentially harmful chemicals.

They use 100 percent recycled waste paper from any number of pre- and post-consumer sources—mostly offices and schools—and convert it to toilet paper, paper towels, and other paper products. Atlas has never cut down a single tree in all the years the company has been in business.

Herbal Lifestyle, in Falls Church, Virginia (www.herballifestyle.com), creates hand-crafted herbal bath and body products made from only natural and organic ingredients. They compost all of the herbs that they use to make infused oils, and they also use compostable cellulose bags for their products rather than plastic.

American Yogini in Jamesport, New York (www.americanyogini.com), is in the fresh juice business and has a LOT of fruit and vegetable pulp to deal with. The fresh vegetable and fruit pulp is composted with their office scrap paper.

When they finish the juicing process and put pulp on the pile, they add their shredded office papers to the bin. The finished compost goes back into the garden where it all started. They also have a teaching garden where they grow some of the vegetables they use in their juice blends.

Digging Deeper

If you have or know of a company that composts its waste or has a compostable product, please send me a short e-mail at (chris@asuburbanfarmer.com) describing how it works and I'll add it to a perpetual "Companies That Compost" page on my website, www.asuburbanfarmer.com.

The Least You Need to Know

- Composting as a neighborhood gives everyone a reason to come together other than as a crime watch.

- Community gardens can be ideal for gathering organic materials into a compost pile.

- Your county is an excellent resource for composting information.

- Visit community compost piles in your neighborhood for ideas and inspiration.

- A number of innovative companies have started composting on a company-wide level.

Glossary

acidic material   Organic materials that fall lower than 7 on the pH (acidic/alkaline) scale of 1 through 14.

actinomycetes   Microorganisms that are half bacteria and half fungi. They do their breakdown work in a compost pile at temperatures ranging from 70°F to 90°F.

activators   Organic materials, usually nitrogen or microorganisms, used to jump-start the decomposition process.

aerate   To add air; in composting, it usually involves turning the pile or adding ventilation stacks.

aerobic   Living or occurring only in the presence of oxygen.

anaerobic   Those processes or organisms that can function without oxygen present.

bacteria   Single-celled microorganisms.

biodegradable   Capable of being broken down by living organisms into a simpler component.

biofertilizer   Many microorganisms that increase the amount of nutrients available to plants.

blood meal   Dried blood that's sometimes used as an activator for compost piles; it is also used as a fertilizer.

broadcast   The act of spreading a soil or plant amendment like fertilizer evenly across any given area. Usually this is done by hand or a hand-held spreading tool.

buffer   Any compound that makes the soil less sensitive to acid and alkaline fluctuations.

C:N ratio   The carbon to nitrogen ratio in an organic substance.

carbon materials   Usually dry materials such as straw, leaves, sawdust, cornstalks, cardboard, and paper. The balance of the C:N (carbon to nitrogen) ratio is 30:1. So if the "C" number of the ratio is higher than 30, they're considered a carbon.

carnivore   Any animal that primarily eats meat or meat-based food.

castings   Organic matter that's been ingested by worms and passed through the worms' guts to become a highly nutritional substance for soil and plants. Also known as vermicastings.

clitellum   Also known as a saddle, the band around the worm that secretes the cocoons that holds the baby worms.

coir   A soil-less plant medium made from the outside fibers of coconuts; it's a sustainable alternative to peat moss. Also called coco-peat or coir-peat.

cold composting   The practice of composting with minimal physical labor. You pile together browns and greens and let them sit until they decompose.

compost   Organic waste that has been biologically reduced to humus. The term is used for both the process and the end product.

compost sandwich   Composting technique involving layering and alternating browns and greens on a site destined to be a garden bed. No turning or adding more materials is involved.

compost tea   Liquid made by "brewing" compost in a cloth; the liquid is then added to the soil or sprayed on plant leaves.

cover crop   A crop that's grown specifically to enrich or protect soil, or to control weeds.

decomposer   Any organism that helps break down dead plant and animal cells.

earth worm   See *nightcrawler.*

fertilize   To supply nutrients to plants.

foundation planting   Plantings around the foundation of a home. Usually the original foundation plantings are planted by the builder, and then sometimes replaced or supplemented by the home owner.

friable soil   Soil with an open structure that crumbles when handled. Also called tilth.

fruit flies   Tiny, gnatlike flies that are attracted to rotting fruit.

fungi (fungus)   A plant that lacks chlorophyll and vascular tissue.

gizzard   Part of a worm's digestive tract located in the anterior portion of the worm's body.

gnats   Small, black, flying insects that love fungus. They don't bite, but they're annoying.

grasscycling   The practice of leaving grass clippings on the lawn after mowing so the nutrients in the clippings can return to the soil.

green manure   Any crop grown for the sole purpose of adding nutritional value to a soil by adding organic matter or nutrients such as nitrogen. Green manures are turned under the soil while they are still green and tender.

hardpan soil   Topsoil that is so hard plant roots can't penetrate the earth. Composting can be the perfect solution for this type of soil.

herbicide   A synthetic chemical substance used to kill weeds.

herbivore   An animal that eats plants or plant-based foods.

hot composting   The practice of keeping a fast-acting compost pile by balancing the browns (carbon), greens (nitrogen), moisture, and oxygen. This makes the temperatures toward the middle of the pile hot, which helps the compost break down quickly.

humus   Material that's formed after the breakdown of organic matter. It makes complex nutrients in the soil easily accessible to plants.

inoculant   Microorganisms such as fungi and bacteria that can be added to a new compost pile to help begin the decomposition process.

insecticides   Natural and synthetic substances that are designed to kill insects.

lasagna gardening   The process of planting directly into a newly built compost sandwich or sheet compost without waiting for them to decompose.

leachate   The product or solution formed by leaching. A product picked up through the leaching of soil, etc.

leaf mold   The dark, earthy material that results from decomposed leaves. It's just about as close to pure humus as you can get.

legume   A plant that captures nitrogen from the atmosphere because of its association with soilborne bacteria.

lime   A calcium compound made from limestone that raises the alkalinity in compost.

macroorganism   Organisms (animals or plants) large enough to be seen with the naked eye.

mesophiles   Bacteria that decomposes organic matter in temperatures between 70°F–90°F.

microorganism   Organisms (animals or plants) that are too small to be seen with the naked eye.

mites   Pale brown or reddish-brown insects shaped like spiders. Easily seen with a hand lens.

mulching mower   A rotary lawn mower that uses revolving blades to cut grass clippings into extra small pieces as it mows. The mower then distributes the clippings evenly back into the lawn.

mycorrhizal   The symbiotic relationship between beneficial fungi and plant roots.

nematodes   Microscopic worms (usually) either free-living or parasitic. Some nematodes are harmful and some are helpful to plants.

nightcrawler   Also called night crawler. Soil-dwelling worm that leads a solitary life and is responsible for the aeration and mixing of soil. Although they do produce castings, they aren't the type of worms kept for vermicomposting.

nitrogen materials   Materials such as grass clippings, green vegetation, manure, fruits, and vegetables that add nitrogen to a compost pile; any material with a "C" number lower than 30.

open compost pile   A compost pile that is not fully contained. It's vulnerable to wildlife.

organic matter   Any material that originates from living organisms, including all animal and plant life whether still living or in any stage of decomposition.

parasites   Organisms that feed off another living organism and offer nothing back to the host's survival.

pasteurize   To expose something to heat long enough to kill specific types of organisms.

pathogens   Disease-producing organisms.

peat moss   A material mined from ancient bogs, it's considered a nonrenewable soil-less medium or mulch for plants.

pesticide   See *insecticide*.

photosynthesis   The process in which plants make their own food by using the sun and converting carbon dioxide and water into glucose (plus other sugars and starches). The waste product plants produce is oxygen.

pot worms   Little white worms that are much smaller than redworms. When found in small numbers in composting systems, they're harmless.

potting soil   A mixed medium used for potting indoor and outdoor plants.

prostomium   A sensitive flap of skin that protrudes above the mouth of a worm that helps the worm find food.

psychrophiles   Bacteria that breaks down organic material in the cooler temperatures of around 55°F.

rabbitry   Rabbit housing; a place where rabbits are bred and raised.

red wigglers   Common term for redworms with the Latin names *Eisenia fetida*, *Lumbricus rubellus*, and *Eisenia andrei*. They're all loosely defined as red wigglers and are ideal for use in a vermicompost system.

reel mower   A human-powered (as opposed to motorized) lawn mower. It works by cutting grass blades with a spinning reel of blades.

scarification   The process of wearing down hard-shelled seeds to aid in germination.

setae   Bristlelike structures on each segment of a worm that help them move along the earth.

sheet composting   See *compost sandwich*.

side-dressing   Nutrients applied to soil near a plant's stems.

soil pH   The acidity or alkalinity of soil; the scale runs from 1 through 14. Soil is in balance when it falls between 6.5 and 7 on the pH scale.

soldier fly larvae   Immature soldier fly maggots (babies). The larvae aren't worm predators, so they won't harm them. But if they become too numerous, they could out-compete them for food.

symbiotic relationship   Situation in which plants or animals of different species live together in a mutually advantageous relationship.

thermophiles   Bacteria that move into a hot pile to work at temperatures between 100°F and 160°F.

top-dressing   A soil amendment such as compost or fertilizer applied evenly over the surface of a garden bed.

toxoplasmosis   A disease often picked up by handling used cat litter, caused by the protozoan *Toxoplasma gondii*.

trench composting Burying organic materials in a trench or hole. This is usually done near or in an existing garden bed.

ventilate To let fresh air into the compost pile. Making holes or gaps so air can circulate.

vermicompost Worm castings mixed with bedding and partially decomposed organic matter (food). Vermicompost includes worms, their cocoons, and whatever else is living in the worm bin.

worm bin Any container used to accommodate a vermicomposting system.

worm condo Commercial vermicomposting systems that work on a two- or three-tiered system.

zone (USDA) The U.S. Department of Agriculture's map dividing the United States into 11 growing areas. It's based on a 10°F difference. Micro-climates within a zone as well as rainfall, day length, humidity, wind, and soil types also play a role in planting specifics. Therefore, the map is meant to be used as a general guide.

Resources

Composting Websites and Blogs

Visit the following websites and blogs for additional resources on building or maintaining your compost bin, pile, or vermicompost systems.

Worm Farming With Fred #422

www.facebook.com/home.php#/group.php?gid=75356045451

The Complete Idiot's Guide to Composting's own "Wise Worm" has a Facebook group on composting for readers to join.

California Integrated Waste Management Board

www.ciwmb.ca.gov/organics/Homecompost/

Visit this site for answers to common home-composting questions.

Composting Blog

http://blog.composters.com

A source for good insights on composting and vermicomposting.

Mama's Worm Composting

www.mamaswormcomposting.com

Excellent site on vermicomposting at home.

Composting in Santa Cruz County

www.compostsantacruzcounty.org

A friendly and informative county composting site.

Equipment and Supplies

The following online retailers sell composting supplies. Some of these sites sell cover crop and green manure seeds, too.

Good Compost
www.goodcompost.com
Look no further for your Soil Saver fully enclosed compost bin or Tumbleweed Compost Tumbler.

Cascade Manufacturing Sales, Inc.
www.cascadewormbin.com
Here's the place to get a classy set-up for your worm farm.

NatureMill, Inc
www.naturemill.com/products.html
Interested in composting right in your kitchen? You'll find cool indoor composting systems at this site.

Fiskars
www.fiskars.com
Here's where you'll find some awesome reel and mulching mowers to get you grasscyling.

Foothill Worm Ranch
www.foothillwormranch.com/
Foothill Worm Ranch will ship your worms right to your front door.

Clean Air Gardening
www.cleanairgardening.com/
Specializes in eco-friendly gardening tools. You'll find a ton of composting and garden supplies here.

Planet Natural
www.planetnatural.com/site/index.html
More Earth-friendly supplies to peruse, along with beneficial insects for the garden.

Peaceful Valley Farm Supply
www.groworganic.com
Online source for organic cover crop and green manure seeds plus much, much more.

Olive Barn
www.olivebarn.com
A nice source for kitchen crocks and pails for holding kitchen scraps until you can get them to the compost bin.

Seeds of Change
www.seedsofchange.com
Another great source for organic cover crop/green manure seeds—plus much more.

Stoney Knoll
www.gardensifters.com
This family-based company is a good source for compost sifters.

Green People
www.greenpeople.org/seeds.htm
Yet another supplier of cover crop and green manure seeds.

Gardener's Supply
www.gardeners.com
You'll find aerating (turning) tools here plus tons of other gardening tools.

Cyndi's Catalog of Garden Catalogs
www.gardenlist.com
The mother lode of gardening catalogs.

Books

The following books are some of the best composting references available.

Campbell, Stu. *Let it Rot!* Storey Publishing, LLC, 1998.
Stu Campbell has been guiding composting gardeners since 1975 with this oldie but goodie.

Appelhof, Mary. *Worms Eat My Garbage*. Flower Press, 1997.
Mary Appelhof's world-renowned worm-farming book is full of great answers.

Lamp'l, Joe. *The Green Gardener's Guide*. Cool Springs Press, 2007.
Here's where you'll get some solid numbers in terms of the incredible impact that composting and other green practices have on our world. A must-read.

Martin, Deborah, and Gershuny, Grace. *The Rodale Book of Composting*. Rodale Press, 1992.
A composting book that's chock full of great ideas.

Lanza, Patricia. *Lasagna Gardening*. Rodale Press, 1998.
This book shows you how you can garden in your compost sandwich right away.

Bubel, Nancy. *The New Seed Starter's Handbook*. Rodale Press, 1988.
Everything you need to know about seeding your cover crop or green manure.

Mays, Howard L. *Raising Fish Worms with Rabbits*. Shields Publications, 1981.
All you ever wanted to know about raising worms for the end of your hook.

Shields, Earl B. *Raising Earthworms for Profit.* Shields Publications, 1994.
Have rabbits? Double up on your profit in the same space you're using right now.

University Extension Offices

University of California
ucanr.org
Numerous links to resources for composting educators.

University of Missouri
extension.missouri.edu
A great source of information on soils and composting.

University of Illinois
web.extension.uiuc.edi/homecompost/history.html
Interesting insights on composting as well as some composting history.

Colorado State University
www.ext.colostate.edu/sam/compost.html
Composting information plus sustainable small acreage topics.

Organizations

U.S. Composting Council
www.compostingcouncil.org
All about composting beyond your backyard.

Association of Compost Producers
www.healthysoil.org
Education on the benefits of composting, backed by quality scientific research.

Washington Organic Recycling Counsel
www.compostwashington.org
All kinds of composting and recycling information plus tons of links to explore.

Cornell Composting
compost.css.cornell.edu/schools.html
An ideal resource for anyone interested in composting in schools or classrooms.

New York State Association for Reduction, Reuse and Recycling
www.nysar3.org
A website dedicated to providing statewide leadership on waste reduction, reuse and recycling issues, and practices to improve the environment.

Compost and Worms in the Classroom

This appendix includes a variety of composting and vermicomposting activities specially designed for the classroom.

These activities aren't limited to traditional school-type classrooms. Home schools and youth organizations such as 4H, Girl Scouts, and Boy Scouts can all adopt these projects for their own use. Or try doing them as a family project at home.

Composting in the Classroom

Bringing composting into the classroom is a valuable teaching tool that introduces important concepts to school-age children. By studying composting, kids learn about such things as the life cycle, death and decomposition, resource management, and the state of our garbage and landfills. You'll also have the opportunity to teach about biodegradable and nonbiodegradable items and how this affects recycling and renewal for the earth.

Not to mention the dirt. The dirt, of course, is the best part of having compost in the classroom. The kids get to put their hands in dirt, make compost piles, play with worms, and analyze what they eat and throw away. In the end, kids will gain a new appreciation for resources and our environment. Plus, this is one of those "side" curriculums that are exceptionally fun to teach.

Biodegradable or Not?

The goal for this activity is to give the kids hands-on experience deciding what is biodegradable (and therefore compostable) and what can and can't be recycled.

Materials needed:

◆ Biodegradable items that might be thrown in the trash

◆ Nonbiodegradable items that might be thrown in the trash

◆ Blackboard and chalk or a large piece of butcher-type paper and markers

For this activity you'll want to have on hand different examples of "trash" such as plastic soda bottles, aluminum foil, paper, grass clippings, food waste, leaves, clothing (100 percent cotton would be compostable), and glass bottles.

You might ask each child to bring in something that he or she has actually thrown away. But you may need to bring in a few items to ensure you have enough examples for each category.

Place all of the garbage-bound items together on one table. Then, using a blackboard or large sheet of paper, ask the students to name things that get thrown away daily at home and at school. Give the kids plenty of time to brainstorm. Feel free to guide them by asking them to think about particular situations, such as holidays (gift wrap comes to mind). Write each item on the chalkboard.

Explain to the class that materials made from things that once lived are biodegradable. Talk about the natural cycle of death, decay (decomposition), and then rebirth as the composted materials support plant and animal life. Ask students to raise their hand if they see anything on the list that's biodegradable and can be added to a compost pile. Have them circle those items.

Then ask a student to go over to the table and remove all the compostable items. Although you have a list going on the board, the physical presence of the items you're talking about hit home for kids much more than just the words on the board.

Next, have a student circle the items on the board that don't actually decompose but can be recycled, such as glass and plastic. Have a different student remove those items from the garbage table. Now look at what's left on the table and on the board. Ask the students if they're surprised at how little is left there to actually "throw away."

Follow up with a discussion on what they can do in their lives to minimize the trash they throw out that ends up in our landfills. Recycling bins and compost piles can be part of this conversation, as can being conscious of the products they use.

Dirt in Our Lunch

This activity is intended to get students to track their lunches back to where they originated from—the soil. By demonstrating that everything we eat goes right back to soil, this activity illustrates just how important it is to have healthy soil. When we simply toss our biodegradable products into a landfill, we waste valuable nutrients that could otherwise be giving new life.

Materials needed:

- ◆ Journals

- ◆ Drawing paper

- ◆ Markers or crayons

- ◆ Kids' lunches

This project works well if students are broken into smaller groups or even pairs. You may want to bring a sample lunch of your own so that you're sure to have a variety of foods.

Ask students to try to name a food that doesn't lead back to soil. Then help students look at the ingredients in every food they have to see how it ends up back in the earth.

For instance, for a tuna fish sandwich …

- ◆ **Bread** is made from wheat, which is grown in soil.

- ◆ **Mayonnaise** is made from eggs, which came from chickens, that ate grains, that were grown in soil.

- ◆ **Pickles** are cucumbers that were grown in soil.

- ◆ **Lettuce** was grown in soil.

- ◆ **Tuna** lived in the ocean and ate smaller fish, which ate plankton. The plankton ate phytoplankton, which got its nutrients from the decomposed bodies of dead plants and animals from the ocean floor.

Next, have the students list everything they have in their lunch. Have them draw pictures of where the food ingredients came from. If they have a sandwich, they might draw a wheat field, and if the sandwich has beef in it, they would draw a cow eating grass. Have each student stand up and share with the rest of the students at least a couple of food items on her list.

To extend this lesson, have the students record their food from all their lunches they eat in a week.

Lunch for the Environment

Much of the garbage that's dumped into landfills can be composted, reused, or recycled. What we buy and how things are packaged have a huge impact on our environment and our garbage situation. By giving students a hands-on view of what can be done, it encourages them to seek out ways on their own to reduce landfill garbage. It also becomes apparent to kids which natural resources were used to make the waste.

Materials needed:

- Large sheet of paper to make a graph

- Lunch and the Environment Worksheets (see below)

- Four bags or buckets labeled "Compost," "Recycle," "Reuse," "Landfill"

- Discarded lunches from the cafeteria or their lunches from home

- Recycled plastic grocery-store bags for gathering lunch stuff (one for each student)

To create the Lunch and the Environment Worksheet, make a simple grid on a blank piece of paper. Label the top of the rows "Item," "Compost," "Recycle," "Reuse," "Landfill," and "Replace With."

Make enough copies of the Lunch and the Environment Worksheet for each student to have several, depending on how many days you'd like to experiment with it and how many lunch items you've chosen to look at. Set the labeled bags or buckets out on top of a tarp.

Before lunch, hand the grocery bags to each student and ask them to bring back *everything* from their lunches. Tell them not to throw anything out until it's been logged in at the classroom. They can even take the discarded lunches from other students they're eating with and bring that back, too.

Make this an ongoing project for five days. When the students come back to the classroom after lunch, they need to fill out their log sheets to include what category the item falls under (compost, recycle, reuse, or landfill). Then have them put the items they have in the appropriate bag or bucket.

Have them rinse things such as small milk cartons to keep odors out of the classroom, and you'll also want some type of a lid for the compost and landfill buckets. Meat or dairy items should be tallied and then taken out of the classroom daily to keep odors to a minimum. Keep some shredded paper or sawdust on hand for the compost bucket. Most of the lunch waste in that bucket will be food, which is a lot of nitrogen and water.

Some of these lunch items will fall under more than one category. Explain that there's a hierarchy to organizing potential garbage. Reducing the amount of packaging is always the best way to start. Reusing any packaging that's already in existence is the next best thing to reducing. Recycling and composting come next on the list. Using the landfill should be seen as a last resort.

At the end of each day, have the students fill in their totals on their worksheets. Use the last column labeled "Replace With" for brainstorming alternative ways to deal with their lunches that brings the solution "up on the hierarchy chain."

For instance, if they have a juice box on their list, this can be recycled. However, if they used a thermos or reusable plastic bottle they would actually "reduce" their lunch waste, which is a better solution than recycling.

To end this activity, let the whole group not only brainstorm ideas for reducing their waste, but also consider what they might have done already during that week to accomplish this. As far as the compost bucket, you've now started a bucket composting system for your classroom and for another activity.

Critters in My Compost

Compost piles and worm bins have various types of animals that help break down organic materials so they can become compost. In other conditions, some of these critters are considered creepy or undesirable to have hanging around. But here in the compost pile, we appreciate their presence and are happy that they decided to take up residence there.

Materials needed:

- Toothpicks
- Newspaper
- Lined paper
- Pencils

- Compost
- Compost Critters pictures and Compost Critters keys (Print one of each for every student.)
- *Reusable or garden gloves

*Always have students wear gloves when handling compost.

The students will be able to see macrobial decomposers such as sow bugs, worms, beetles, and centipedes. Tell the students how they help decompose organic matter into smaller pieces so microbial decomposers, such as bacteria and fungi, can finish the job. Although too small to see with the naked eye, make sure students are aware that microbial decomposers are always present.

Remind students that without these decomposers, life would cease altogether on this planet. Explain how these animals decompose the organic matter they find and turn it into soil and nutrients in a form that the plants can take up from their roots. Tell them all about the many benefits of compost for plants and soil that you learned in this book.

Make the connection clear so the students can see the vital role these animals play in the life cycle.

If you don't have any compost on hand, get in touch with a gardener who does and ask if you can have a 5-gallon bucket of his soil to borrow for the day. In this activity, you might want the students to work in groups of four, with each one having her own Critter Picture page.

Next, hand out the two worksheets, pencils, and a set of plastic gloves to every student. Have them assemble into groups of four at a table. Have them put the gloves on. Choose one person from each group to come and get one toothpick per student and a pile of compost. Don't forget to explain that the compost they're touching was once leaves, coffee grounds, food waste, and grass clippings before the decomposers got hold of it.

Have the compost handler place a pile of compost onto some newspaper in the center of the table. Now have the students go through the compost carefully with the toothpicks looking for decomposers. Have them check off the critters on their list as they find them.

It counts if other people in their group find them, too. The Compost Critter key will help them properly identify the animals they find in their compost pile. After about 10 minutes, collect the compost and have the groups share what they found in their piles.

Compost Critter Key

◆ **Sow Bug**—This is a grayish isopod with 10 legs. It's about ½ inch long and needs to live in a damp place as it breathes with gills. It likes to eat leaves and other vegetation.

◆ **Fruit Fly**—A very small fly that doesn't bite or sting. They hang around worm bins when food isn't buried properly. They like to lay their eggs in warm, wet places. They won't harm worms.

◆ **Roly Poly (Pill Bug)**—Another dark-gray isopod that resembles an armadillo. They eat veggie scraps and old leaves.

◆ **Centipede**—These worm eaters have 15 to 137 segments to their bodies with a pair of legs on each segment. They are 1 to 2 inches long and usually reddish brown.

◆ **Ant**—An insect with six legs that helps with the decomposition of organic materials. They make soil into clumps and dig tunnels, too.

◆ **Spider**—Spiders have eight legs and are related to mites. Most of them are extremely handy to have in the garden because they control pests that bother plants.

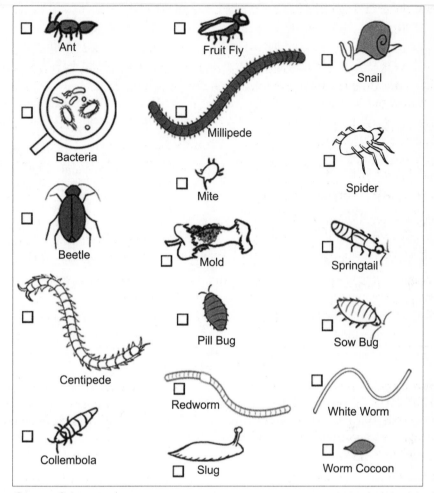

Compost Critters.

- **Snail or Slug**—These are mollusks that look like a snail without its shell. They usually dine on living plant material, but once in a while they'll be attracted to fresh garden trimmings and check out the worm bin or compost pile. The main difference between a slug and a snail is that the snail carries a shell on its back.

- **Springtail**—These white critters are less than $\frac{1}{16}$ inch long and can spring into the air. They eat decaying material and mold.

- **Beetle**—This bug is shiny black and about $\frac{1}{2}$ inch long. It has wings and eats slugs, snails, and caterpillars. You'll find them underneath things like rocks in damp places.

continues

continued

- **Millipede**—This very shy critter is 3 inches long, dark red, and has several legs. He eats soft, decaying plants.

- **Mold**—Mold is related to mushrooms and is a fungus that helps with decomposition. You'll find it on old food such as cheese. Sometimes you'll find it on bread that's been in your house for too long.

- **Mite**—Mites are tiny round critters with eight legs. They are white or brown and eat soft plant material and mold. It would take 25 of these critters to cover a line an inch long.

- **White worm**—This worm is an inch long and looks like a piece of thread. It's a relative of the earthworm and eats rotting food.

- **Bacteria**—Colorless and much too tiny to see with human eyes, bacteria live everywhere. They eat almost anything.

- **Worms**—Worms are long and thin with little segments making up their bodies. They don't have eyes, ears, or legs. They eat decaying food materials, bacteria, and fungi. They are perfect residents in a compost pile.

- **Worm cocoon**—Worm cocoons are shaped like a lemon and are usually clear or yellowish before they hatch. After the baby worms hatch, the cocoon turns green.

Bucket Compost

If you don't have the opportunity to build a compost pile outside with your students, bring the compost pile into the classroom in a bucket.

Materials needed:

- Compostable materials—a mix of both browns and greens

- 5-gallon bucket with a lid

- 1 gallon of finished compost

- Water

- Garden trowel for mixing

- Small tarp for under bucket

Here's your chance to recycle the compost bucket from the "Lunch for the Environment" activity. If you're worried that the food will get smelly in a small classroom, just start from scratch and begin with nonfood ingredients such as yard clippings, paper, and the like.

To begin this project, have students write down a random list of greens or browns they can bring from home. To keep odors down, it'll work in your favor if you add more browns than greens. It'll compost slower, but because you'll be composting indoors it's better to err on the side of too much carbon than too much nitrogen.

Have the students add browns and greens (remember: more browns than greens) until the bucket is about half full. Now add a gallon of finished compost to act as an activator. If you don't have access to finished compost, add sawdust or potting soil.

Keep the materials inside moist, but not truly wet. Have the students write down some predictions such as how long it will take to decompose, what they think it'll smell like while it's decomposing, and if they think they'll find things growing in it.

Every few days, open up the bucket and mix the ingredients. Don't do it more often than this because the microbial decomposers need to settle a bit to break things down. Every two weeks have the students look and observe what's happening inside the compost bucket. Have them record their observations.

As a class, take the finished compost to a planter box or landscape area on the school grounds and place it underneath the plants.

Build a Compost Pile

If there's any way to swing it, see if your classroom can start a compost pile or bin on the school grounds.

Materials needed:

- Compostable materials—both browns and greens
- Compost bin
- Water
- Turning tool

- Hand-held pruning shears
- Handout for building and maintaining a compost pile (1 set per student)
- Garden gloves

Go over the essentials of composting with the students, including the main four ingredients in a pile (carbon, nitrogen, air, and water). If the timing is right and you turn the pile regularly, your students may get a chance to use the compost as early as four to five months from building the pile.

If it doesn't work out that way, whomever you are teaching when it's ready will benefit from seeing the compost at work on plants. At that point, you can either have students use the compost on plants grown at the school, or let them take some home for their own gardens.

Worms in the Classroom

If you consider how much kitchen waste the average family produces in a week, just think about the vast amounts of food and paper produced by schools in that same period. Even if the school recycles their paper products, uneaten food represents the largest category of waste that goes into our landfills.

Having a worm bin in the classroom is an ideal way for teachers to integrate many biological and environmental lesson plans into their curriculum. These lessons are perfect for traditional classrooms as well as home schools and youth organizations such as 4H, Girl Scouts, and Boy Scouts.

Preparing for Worms

The first lesson plan might be to have the students do some brainstorming. Pose the question, "What is vermicomposting?" Have everyone write down their own definition.

Next, break the classroom into three separate groups. Have each group decide on a "team name" that refers to vermicomposting in some way, such as Team Red Wigglers, Team Tiger Worms, and Team Nightcrawlers. Let them keep those group names for the duration of the curriculum.

Have the groups section off and come up with the most common questions about vermicomposting. Expect to hear the following types of questions: Do all worms make vermicompost? How do they make the castings? Are there boy and girl worms? Do worms have teeth? Can they see? Can worms feel? How long do worms live? Are they all the same length? Then split up the questions and assign each group their own set to research and then share their findings with the rest of the class.

Discuss with the class what needs to be done to prepare for the vermicomposting system. Topics to discuss include the types of worms needed for efficient vermicomposting, plans for the worm bin, and a maintenance list. Prepare handouts for the kids to take home and share with their families.

To start a worm composting program with kids in a classroom situation, it pays off to give everybody a role in the activities even if you have to give a role to a small group. The varying roles could be planners, food collectors, worm wranglers, worm feeders, etc.

Another possible activity is to have the students draw a diagram of their proposed worm bin complete with lines separating sections within the bin. These sections would represent the areas that students will be placing the worm food (food waste) and could easily fit into a math curriculum with fractions if they were to measure the sections before they drew them.

Researching the Vermicomposting Cycle

During the research part of the curriculum, give each team small amounts of dampened newspaper, soil, grass clippings, sand, and maybe a slice of fresh apple (you don't want them to handle rotten food).

Next, ask the groups to try and create something similar to castings with the items you've provided giving them about 20 minutes to try. When time is up, ask a spokesperson from each group to explain their findings to the other groups in the class.

Be sure you've gone over the different types of worms that live in the soil. Discuss which worms work the best in vermicompost systems and what role the other types of worms play in the ecosystem. Ideally, have one of the teams research this and bring back information for the rest of the class.

Have the three teams draw an illustration showing how to build and create a vermicompost system and how it all cycles. Remind them to include each part of the process, including the end stages when the castings are added to the soil, vegetables growing in the soil, and people harvesting and eating the food.

Ask the students to come up with different ways a vermicompost system could work, such as the worm boxes under rabbit cages. Let them get as far out as they'd like; it's how great things are invented.

Observing Worms

Assign a different pair of students each day to observe the worms' activity as well as what happens to the food waste and record their observations in a classroom-wide worm journal. Be sure the students put their name by their observations.

Have two students each week collect a small sample of vermicompost and look at it either under a microscope or magnifying lens. Have the students report their findings to the rest of the class.

Worms like cool temperatures in their bins, so have a thermometer taped inside the worm bin to observe and record bin conditions. Keeping record of temperatures can be graphed, which is another great time to incorporate math curriculum.

While the students watch for the appropriate time to add a spritz of water to the worm bin, they can record an approximate time frame that things begin to dry out.

In addition, have the students record how fast the worms ingest the food and how often students need to feed them. This can be made into a group activity by assigning each team a specific thing to record and then have teams each make a graph of their observations to share with the class at the end of the project.

Based on their observations, have the students identify which foods the worms "liked" (ate the fastest) after several weeks. Also talk about which foods the worms left for last. Brainstorm why this might be the case (food too acidic, spicy, etc.).

Worm Lab

Many kids find the lab activities the best part of this project. Worms look like such simple creatures, but there are many things about them you can have the students explore. Before having the students begin to observe and handle the worms, explain that worms are living creatures and, as such, should be treated with respect.

If some kids are squeamish about handling worms, be sure there are some more adventurous worm wranglers on their team. Explain that worms breathe through their skin while its wet and that's why they should be moist at all times during the lab work. The worms can be placed on a wet paper towel or a small dish (like a petri) with a *little* water. If the worms are actually submerged in water they will drown.

Set up lab stations for the kids to rotate through so everyone has a chance to observe, think about, and answer questions. One possible overall topic for a worm lab is "What do you really know about worms?" From there, stations could be set up at different tables with the appropriate observation tools at each one.

A great way to begin lab time is to give the students a hand lens and ask them to get very close up and personal with their worm. Now tell them to try to figure out which is the front end and how do they know this?

Stations could include:

+ **Do worms have eyes? How do they react to light? Why?**

   Darken the room and have the students shine a light on the worm. How does it react? Now have the students put a piece of red cellophane in front of the light beam coming from the flashlight. How did the worms react this time?

   Worms react to light by turning away or burying themselves in their bedding. Worms aren't sensitive to light that is from the red end of the light spectrum, therefore won't react to light streaming through red cellophane. Many nocturnal animals have the same reaction to the red end of the spectrum.

+ **Do worms like water?**

   Have students put a drop of water on a dish or a piece of paper near the worm. What does the worm do? Usually, the worm will wriggle over to the water. Have the students try it when the worm is in a small, dark box—do they get the same results?

◆ **Do worms feel?**

Have students place a worm on a wet paper towel and then touch the worm with a feather or paintbrush. How does the worm react? Are there signs that he has "feeling" receptors? Is it safe to say that worms have senses?

◆ **Which way do worms travel?**

With the worm on a moist paper towel, have the students gently touch one end of the worm with the bristles of a small paintbrush. Did the worm move? Now have them touch the opposite end. Does a worm move forward and backward? Or just forward?

Discuss with them how the worms might actually move. Do the students have any good guesses?

◆ **Do worms prefer one color over another?**

This is a variation of the effect that light has on worms. Using a flashlight again, have the students shine the light through a prism onto a white piece of paper. Now, place the worm in the middle of the spectrum of light on the paper. How does the worm react to each color?

He should crawl away from the blue color and right through the red.

◆ **Do worms like being around other worms?**

When two worms are put next to each other in a container with a lid (the light needs to be blocked out) what happens? Do they move away from each other or towards one another? If they move towards each other are there any guesses as to why? (Are they in love? Need more moisture? What?) If they did the same thing with nightcrawlers, the response may be different.

◆ **What's the average length of a worm?**

Have the students measure several worms to get the average length of a worm. Remind them that the more worms they measure, the more accurate that estimate is going to be.

There are many ways to finish up your classroom vermicomposting project. One of them is to put together a case study where each student writes his or her report based on personal observations and class discussions.

You could also have the students do a group report.

Another final project idea is to have each team take one aspect of the vermicomposting cycle and produce a report of that angle and create a poster along with it. Each group could present it to the classroom.

Go on a field trip to a working worm farm where they raise and supply worms to the public. Don't forget to hand out copies of how to make a worm bin for students to take home.

If you'd like more information on a composting curriculum, contact your cooperative extension office in your county. The National Gardening Association has many kits available for student teaching in their magazine *Gardening With Kids* (www.gardeningwithkids.org).

Index

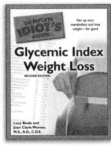

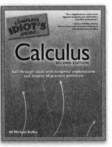